DONALD WINDHAM

Donald Windham, in the Garden of the Monsters, Bomarzo, Rome, photograph by Sandy Campbell, circa 1972

DONALD WINDHAM

A Bio-Bibliography

BRUCE KELLNER

With a Footnote by Donald Windham

Bio-Bibliographies in American Literature,
Number 2

GREENWOOD PRESS
New York • Westport, Connecticut • London

Library of Congress Cataloging-in-Publication Data

Kellner, Bruce.
    Donald Windham : a bio-bibliography / Bruce Kellner ; with a
footnote by Donald Windham.
        p.   cm.—(Bio-bibliographies in American literature, ISSN
0742-695X ; no. 2)
    Includes index.
    ISBN 0-313-26857-6 (alk. paper)
    1. Windham, Donald—Bibliography.   I Title.   II. Series.
[PS3573.I5]
016.813'54—dc20   91-10777

British Library Cataloguing in Publication Data is available.

Library of Congress Catalog Card Number: 91-10777
ISBN: 0-313-26857-6
ISSN: 0742-695X

First published in 1991

Greenwood Press, 88 Post Road West, Westport, CT   06881
An imprint of Greenwood Publishing Group, Inc.

Printed in the United States of America

The paper used in this book complies with the
Permanent Paper Standard issued by the National
Information Standards Organization (Z39.48-1984).

10 9 8 7 6 5 4 3 2 1

The author and publisher gratefully acknowledge Donald Windham for
granting permission to use his "Footnote from a Would-be Lop-Eared
Rabbit" and his illustrations, copyright © 1991 by Donald Windham.

In Memoriam

Sandy Montgomery Campbell
1922–1988

The immense proportion of our
intellectual possessions
consists of our delitescent
cognitions.
—Sir William Hamilton

There is probably no hell for
authors in the next world—
they suffer so much from critics
and publishers in this one.
—C. N. Bove

I try to write about reality.
The belief that reality bears
being portrayed seems to me
the only optimism.
—Donald Windham

Contents

Illustrations

Frontispiece

> Donald Windham, in the Garden of the Monsters, Bomarzo, Rome, photograph by Sandy Campbell, circa 1972

Following page 28

> "The Warm Country," 1940, manuscript page with holograph suggestions by Tennessee Williams
>
> **The Warm Country**, 1960, dust jacket design by Heather Standring
>
> **Emblems of Conduct**, 1963, title page design by W. Ferro
>
> **Tanaquil**, 1972, original lithograph wrapper by Tony Smith, numbered and signed by the artist
>
> **Stone in the Hourglass**, 1981, page proof with corrections by Donald Windham

Acknowledgments

In compiling this bibliography, I have
worked directly from Donald Windham's own collection and papers. I am grateful to him for
his sly "Footnote from a Would-be Lop-eared
Rabbit" to my introduction; but I am also
grateful to him for his patience with my questions, for his attention to details, for his
objectivity over my editorial decisions and
opinions, for permission to quote from his
published and unpublished writings, and to
reproduce illustrations connected with his work.
Surely I am even more grateful for our warm
friendship that even collaboration has not
marred.

I am also indebted to the reference staff
of Ganser Library, at Millersville University
where I teach, for its persistence in tracking
down fugitive reviews; to the Millersville
University Faculty Development Program for a
research grant in 1989 and for a one-quarter
release time grant during the 1990 fall semester
so I could complete the manuscript; to the
University of Georgia Library for supplying
copies of Windham's juvenilia from his high
school newspaper; to the Philadelphia Free
Library for its remarkable microfilm collection
through which I was able to trace a number of
obscure references.

Minor services invariably make major contributions: my thanks to my editor Marilyn
Brownstein for agreeing to endorse this project;

to my associates at Millersville University, Phillip Shaak for lessons at the laser, Christina Lohr not only for preparing the copy for print but for its indexing, Joanne Demming and Kay Foutz for library sleuthing, and James Yescalis for illustrations. The oldest appellation in scholarly acknowledgments, "friend and colleague," regains all its luster because of Timothy Miller; his patience with this late-comer to word processors was exemplary. Finally, I must thank two old friends: Richard Rutledge, for bed and board during periods of research on this and earlier scholarly undertakings; and Priscilla Oppenheimer, who has been as always an unerringly honest, perceptive, and helpful reader.

Introduction: In Defense of Delitescence

For fifty years, Donald Windham has been quietly building a body of work, modest in quantity but substantial by any measure connected with arts and letters. E. M. Forster's observation, in his introduction to **The Warm Country**, is worth repeating: "Mr Windham, I understand, has never learnt literature. He merely produces it" (1).

Donald Windham has written five novels, at least three of which are exemplars of their especial subjects, the other two of considerable interest if less satisfying by comparison. His stories are explosions in closets, as unexpected as a stranger's handclasp that seems somehow familiar, and they have been compared favorably and in detail by more than one perceptive reviewer to James Joyce's stories in **The Dubliners**. His memoir of his boyhood, **Emblems of Conduct**, belongs on that shelf of similar rarities, books that evoke a common innocence despite their variety in setting and experience, and recreate both the sweetness and the sorrow in growing up: Donald Hall's **String Too Short to be Saved**, Edwin Muir's **The Story and the Fable**, Sacheverell Sitwell's **All Summer in a Day**, Gerald Lord Berners's **First Childhood**, and Curtis Harnack's **We Have All Gone Away**, for example, or, more recently, the early chapters in Jill Kerr Conway's **The Road from Coorain** or James Chace's **What We Had**. Perhaps Windham has read none of these books; perhaps their authors

still living never read **Emblems of Conduct**. No
matter: the books are all indelible biographies
of their readers as well as autobiographies of
their writers whose backgrounds share nothing at
all but the anguish common in coming of age.
Windham's later memoirs, or later autobiographical studies, **As if . . .** and **Footnote to a
Friendship**, are painful but luminously intelligent as well as compassionate assessments of the
devastating effects of public persona on private
lives.

From the publication of **The Dog Star** in
1950 through **Lost Friendships** in 1988, Windham
has always enjoyed the endorsements of significant literary figures, not only Forster, but also
J.R. Ackerley, Paul Bowles, Albert Camus, Andre
Gide, Harper Lee, Thomas Mann, James Merrill,
Marianne Moore, Georges Simenon, Carl Van Vechten, and, before their descent into celebrity,
Truman Capote and Tennessee Williams.

But commercial publishers have long been
indifferent to his work, and too often hasty
journalists and reviewers have dismissed his
subtlety which is in part his singular virtue: a
prose narrative so uncluttered and so con-
trolled, and with a deliberate eye for telling
detail, that the immediate effect can lead to
impatience. In **Emblems of Conduct**, Windham said
he liked books he wanted to reread more than he
wanted to reread books that he liked (174); it
is not surprising, then, that he writes for
those who share that predilection. "Where is he
going?" readers hyped on the speed of pop culture are likely to ask, since social climate and
fast action do not often intrude on Windham's
fiction to any marked degree. To complicate the
matters of the marketplace -- commercial or
literary -- Donald Windham's subject is almost
invariably sexual but it is never erotic. Ever
since some people began reading D. H. Lawrence
and Henry Miller for the wrong reasons, it has
become increasingly difficult for a writer to
employ the subject for the right ones. Questions of right and wrong, of course, are only
relative, but pornography is readily available
now, and cheap, and quicker than anything
Lawrence or Miller ever had to offer. Readers
anticipating thrills from Windham because of the
explicitness they have come to expect from that

same pop culture, hastening very nearly everything, will find their impatience and disappointment giving way to indifference.

One other matter accounts for Windham's
failure to find an audience. He is a homosexual
author, or, rather, his books have homosexual
characters in them, but never either to
titillate or to commiserate over a subject all
too often employed for one or the other purpose.
Until fairly recently in our literary history,
homosexuality was often avoided or disguised by
writers and dismissed by the bulk of reviewers
in prestigious publications. Windham is not the
only writer whose work has suffered as a result.
Obscurity and celebrity may as well be synony-
mous: the deliberate neglect of Henry Blake
Fuller's remarkable novel, **Bertram Cope's Year**,
published in 1919, for example; the initial
response to the later novels of Christopher
Isherwood; the scholarly discourse brought to
bear on Thomas Mann's **Death in Venice**, seemingly
to avoid rather than face its subject. Until
the current generation, some laborers in the
American sector of the academic community simply
did not grasp, or pretended they did not grasp,
what Walt Whitman and Herman Melville and Hart
Crane were writing about. Were Whitman's early
failure and Melville's later one subliminally
influenced by the homophobia that still afflicts
our culture? Even in 1991, more than one
thickly impressive American literature anthology
skirts this crucial issue in Hart Crane's work.

For widely varying reasons in addition to
these that may account for Donald Windham's lack
of readers, the list of writers who have been
overlooked or underread during the time of their
careers is as substantial as it is distin-
guished. Nor is Windham's name likely to mark
the end of it.

Despite "the depressing consistency" of the
circumstance, Carl Van Vechten wrote in **Excavations**, his 1926 collection of essays about overlooked writers, "I still wax melancholy when I
recall how many literary reputations lie buried
in America, a country which seems to derive a
perverse pleasure from indulgence in necrophilic
auctorial amours -- the longer the bones have
bleached the better" (129). Edgar Allan Poe,
Ambrose Bierce, Edgar Saltus, and Gertrude

Stein, as well as Melville, Whitman, and Fuller,
figured notably in his catalog, writers of
vastly unequal merit, but all vindicated by
time, not only through expensive "Books for
Libraries" reprints but in some instances
through their having taken up residence on the
classroom's Parnassus. Who read Kate Chopin's
The Awakening, in or out of the classroom, until
its relatively recent acknowledgment?   The list
can be extended easily with names of more recent
writers whose fiction and non-fiction have been,
or still are, overlooked or underread for a
number of reasons. How many readers did William
Faulkner have during the twenty productive years
of his career prior to 1945 when he was finally
widely acknowledged? Even at the beginning of
his career, Faulkner had more readers than
Gertrude Stein ever enjoyed. She made no money
from her writing until she was pushing sixty,
and when she was sixty-one, at the zenith of her
celebrity, her **Geographical History of America**
sold fewer than 200 of its 1000 copies; her
publisher seems to have pulped the rest. Now
Stein has become a literary cottage industry.
The classic case is older: for nearly seventy-
five years after its failure on publication,
Melville's **Moby Dick** sold for fifty cents a copy
in second-hand book-shops.
    Bibliographies are unlikely to sell a
writer's books; this one is equally unlikely to
create an audience for the brief bookshelf that
the work of Donald Windham occupies. Still,
when in time the patient reader who cares about
the kind of quiet eloquence associated with the
writings of, say, E. M. Forster discovers Windham's books, it will be good to have a clear
record to account for his development as a
writer, his critical reception, his failures,
and his achievements.
    Donald Windham is a southern writer only by
birth; not even in his boyhood memoir, **Emblems
of Conduct**, written when he was about forty and
published in 1963, is there any suggestion of
the ripe tricks usually associated with that
gothic territory which has so enriched our
literature. Few looney eccentrics populate his
fiction, and there is no racial angst, although
Windham included events from his family history
and other youthful experiences from time to time

in his early work. Further, from the beginning,
his manner has been more European than American:
deliberate, cool, exact. Donald Windham was
born in Atlanta, Georgia, 2 July 1920, and he
left there as soon as he could.

The second son of Fred and Louise Donaldson
Windham, he was raised by his mother following
her divorce when he was six years old, and
brought up in his grandparents' house, a late
Victorian structure with faded gables and
cupolas that kept pace with the family's descent
into poverty. A sprawling roster of relatives
came and went in what was called the "homeplace," where Windham's mother and one of her
sisters lived with their children. But their
genuine penury eventually led their relatives to
sell the house, which was in joint ownership,
a legacy from their parents. The sisters then
moved into separate cramped quarters where Windham endured his adolescence, impatient but tolerant of his impractical mother, and alienated
from his older brother.

Windham graduated from high school with an
undistinguished record, having pursued a private
curriculum of his own devising that embraced a
broad representation of writers, sequentially
from Saroyan to Huxley to Proust to Joyce to
Stein to Silone, and then returning to writers
who had gone before. His concern when he began
to read, he later reflected in **Emblems of Conduct**, was nothing he wished to explain to anyone
else:

> What you need to explain to yourself is
> what reality is. . . . And although this
> amounts to explaining your viewpoint to
> yourself, it is an act that changes your
> viewpoint in the process. Not until you
> have finished do you know what you are
> doing. (168-69)

After graduation, Windham took a few life
drawing classes. He began to write a little.
He started spending time with some members of
Atlanta's nearest equivalent to Bohemia. He met
Fred Melton, a young graphic artist with whom he
has remained close friends. He had no idea of
where he was headed except that he did not look
forward to being promoted to an office job from

the warehouse in which he made barrels and
hauled them around in the local Coca-Cola fac-
tory for a year and a half. His mother envi-
sioned a promotion as upward mobility; Windham
saw it only as another cell from which to look
out on Georgia's limited horizon. These early
experiences gave him material for some short
stories eventually, reflected with devastating
irony, for example, in one about a poseur's
escape from small-town frustrations by running
away to the big city, and in more than one con-
fronting racial stereotypes. No writer ever
entirely escapes the influence of his upbringing
on his work; it will always haunt his margins,
even if he flees it at his first opportunity.
When Donald Windham was nineteen he left for New
York with Fred Melton, ostensibly for a week's
vacation, and never returned.

For the next three years, he and Melton
shared a series of addresses, even for a time
after Melton married. He worked at a number of
odd jobs, including -- in a coincidence that
fiction could support only with difficulty --
dispensing Coca-Cola during the summer of 1940
at the World's Fair that had opened in New York
the previous year. He began to write stories
about his past in Atlanta. During this same
period he came to know Tennessee Williams, a
significant figure in his life and his work,
although as often for ill as for good, for over
forty years. Williams was his senior by nearly
a decade, the first person he had ever met whose
commitment to writing was inviolable. At about
the same time, Windham met a number of artists
in many mediums: Paul Cadmus, Anne Ryan, Jared
French, Tony Smith, and Fritz Bultman; ballet
impresario Lincoln Kirstein; Christopher
Isherwood; Glenway Wescott. A few years later,
he added Truman Capote to his circle of friends,
although in time the long friendships with
Williams and Capote would become the **Lost
Friendships** of Windham's most recent memoir.

In early 1942, he and Williams worked
together on a dramatization of D. H. Lawrence's
story, "You Touched Me," subsequently produced
professionally, which Windham had begun writing
before they met. A few months later, he began
work on his first novel, **The Dog Star**, a clear-
eyed biography of a boy for whom society --

within the modest limitations that his vision of
it allows -- has failed. Loosely modelled on
the life and death of Fred Melton's older
brother, **The Dog Star** is constructed on the
Actaeon myth, in which a brave boy unwittingly
spies on the goddess Artemis, or Diana, and is
transformed into a vulnerable stag and destroyed
by his own hounds. **The Dog Star** pits Blackie
Pride against an alien world that he ultimately
rejects through suicide. Both the subject
matter and narrative would have seemed more
shocking in 1950 when the novel was published
than they now do: Blackie is only fifteen but
sexually active, by turns indifferent and
vicious, but the actual telling is implacably
calm and bereft of either sentimentality or
sensationalism. Several years in its making,
The Dog Star is an often painful example of what
Windham later referred to as writing about
reality. It is fiction so unerringly accurate
that its skill may be hampered by its
relentlessness, although that was not achieved
immediately when Windham began the book in the
summer of 1942. He wrote then as he writes now,
slowly; indeed, "writes" may be a less
appropriate verb to apply to the process than
"makes," a perpetual revising.

In October he went to work as Lincoln
Kirstein's assistant on **Dance Index**, that
remarkable periodical from the early forties
that documented both ballet and modern dance in
America, featuring new material on the contemporary scene and reprinting long-forgotten
reviews and criticism as well as documentary
photographs. Even now, when dance has finally
emerged as a popular art form with a wide public, **Dance Index** remains an invaluable source of
information for students and scholars. When
Kirstein went into the army in March 1943, Windham became editor and turned out the issues
himself. In the process of serving as secre-
tary, writer, checker, errand boy, and proof-
reader, all at Kirstein's urging, he enlarged
his circle of acquaintances to include several
contributors to the magazine: Pavel Tchelitchew, about whose theater and ballet designs he
wrote for one issue, photographer George Platt
Lynes, and collagist Joseph Cornell who contributed illustrations, all three of whom

figured long afterward in Windham's novel
Tanaquil; also George Balanchine, whose essay
made up of "Notes" about ballet choreography
Windham ghost-wrote by taking notes on Balanchine's ideas, then revising them to his
criticisms through successive drafts.

Many of the people Windham met after his
arrival in New York -- most of them at the
outsets of their own careers -- were in various
ways influential on his formative period as a
writer, but none so profoundly as Sandy Campbell. As a freshman at Princeton University,
later to become a professional actor and editor,
Campbell met Windham by chance in October 1942,
and again, through Paul Cadmus, the following
spring. A remarkable symbiosis developed
between them, professional as well as emotional,
fostering Windham's writing, and surely sustain-
ing him through long periods when publishers and
editors seemed largely indifferent to his work.
Markedly different in temperament -- outwardly
at least -- and at the same time fully attuned
to each other's talents and respectful of them,
Windham and Campbell were partners in a strong
and productive relationship until the latter's
unexpected death in 1988. During their forty-
five years together, Windham's novels and memoirs came to birth in a rare collaboration.

The modest success of **You Touched Me!** in
the fall of 1945 allowed Windham to devote himself fully to his writing, not only further
short stories but also his nearly perpetually
revised **The Dog Star.** In 1948 he went to Italy for
the first time, completed the novel, and stayed on
because living expenses were cheap then. An
agent spent nine months trying to place the
novel without success; when Windham returned to
America, it was accepted by Doubleday, the first
publisher to whom he submitted it himself.

Before **The Dog Star** appeared in print,
Windham wrote a second novel, titled in manuscript "Like a Flower," but it has not been
published. Many years later he incorporated
some of its content into his fourth novel, **Tanaquil**, but his next published work was **The Hero
Continues.** This narrative, loosely based on the
career of Tennessee Williams and including some
incidents from their early friendship, is a disturbing study of the thin line between integrity

and disintegration. The ironically named
"human" Denis Freeman becomes the "hero" Denis,
private man becoming public icon. In the process he loses his ability for love and friendship, paralleled through physical losses -- an
eye, an arm, finally the onset of impotence
simultaneously physical and psychosomatic. The
distinction between human and hero is clearly
drawn: one cannot be both; for the hero to continue as a writer, he must of necessity divest
himself of much that makes him human, a sour
view perhaps but an accurate one for Windham's
playwright, although the novel's conclusion
suggests it may be possible to escape the
artist's dilemma and continue as a writer.

In later work, Windham wrote directly and
with appalling accuracy of the dangers of
public success in America, having seen its
ravages in Tennessee Williams and Truman Capote.
His memoirs of his relationships with them, **As
if . . .** and **Footnote to a Friendship,** illustrate with grace and some grief what critic
Robert Ferro observed about Windham a few years
ago, in 1983:

> He has always lived in the shadow of his
> better-known friends, Tennessee and Truman,
> whose last names, through fame, one need
> not list. But through the exigencies of
> drugs, liquor and celebrity, it seems the
> time for their contributions is over, while
> Mr. Windham, who perhaps came in with a
> marble or two less, still has all of his
> and happily many years more to display his
> prodigious gifts (13).

Moreover, in the role of reviewer himself, Windham has been consistently clear-eyed, predicat-
ing his criticism on the factual record that all
too often has eluded some biographers of his
celebrated friends. The reviews -- like his
infrequent letters to the editors -- are invariably informative, in correcting the published
record, often funny, and sometimes too wickedly
intelligent to encourage rejoinders in "Letters
to the Editor" columns.

The same year that **The Hero Continues** was
published, 1960, Windham was awarded a Guggenheim Fellowship in creative writing in fiction,

through which he spent a year in Greece, Denmark, England, and finally in Italy, where he worked on further autobiographical pieces that would eventually develop into **Emblems of Conduct**, and he amassed the material that led to his next novel, **Two People**. Also, in 1960, he collected a number of his stories as **The Warm Country**. Several of these had appeared in various foreign periodicals -- **Horizon**, **Paris Review**, **Botteghe Oscure**, for example -- during the late forties and fifties, but few in America. Published only in England until two years later when the book found an American publisher, the stories occur primarily in Georgia, with two or three excursions to Italy, and the characters are almost always feckless or desperate, sometimes both, locked into suffocating circumstances of their own invention: a frightened bigot, a foolish dilettante, a bewildered policeman, a boy who in frustration beats up a girl, an Italian-American wrestling with his heritage, a suppressed spinster, a woman intimidated into loneliness and eccentricity by a sibling's diffidence and even cruelty. Little happens but to remind the reader of Thoreau's familiar observation that most of us "lead lives of quiet desperation."

Had Windham written nothing further, however, his eventual place in American literature might have been assured because of "The Starless Air," a story that may be described with impunity as a southern parados of Joyce's early masterpiece, **The Dead**. "The Starless Air" may be Windham's own masterpiece, less powerful than Joyce's story, but nevertheless a deeply moving account of a Christmas dinner staged in desperation against the genteel decay of an impoverished Atlanta family. The texture of the story is probably impossible to illustrate with a passage taken out of context, but this reflection, so freighted with what is unspoken, may serve:

> Standing in the bay of windows beside her Christmas tree, Lois looked out at the unpierced night sky. Snow had begun to fall. Slowly, the ornaments of the boarding house across the street were outlined in white and the house itself disappeared

against the black sky. And suddenly she
was crying without thinking why, crying as
though the cause of her grief lay in the
cold window glass and their yard, the water
faucet wrapped in crocus sacking, and the
buildings disappearing in the snow. Toward
the snow of falling cornices and fading
spindles she felt the fear which she had
felt toward strange places and people not
her kind. In the white disappearing of
gables and mansards, the walls of the
homeplace dissolved and left her bare to
the world. All the things which she loved
had come from that world: her children; her
diamonds rings and pearshaped buttons; the
ornaments on the tree at her side, saved
year after year since the first Christmas
of her marriage. But she had thought that
she would never leave the homeplace again,
that she and her children would stay here
always with the many people death had
undone in the house, and she did not understand what had happened. (72-73)

Windham dramatized "The Starless Air" for a
production in Houston in 1953. Tennessee Williams directed it, and the Theatre Guild took an
option, but it was never produced in New York.
Also, Windham dramatized **The Angelic Avengers**,
the Baroness Karen Blixen's gothic romance published not under her familiar pseudonym "Isak
Dinesen" but as the work of "Pierre Andrezel."
It was optioned for a professional production as
well, but that too fell through.
   A third novel, **Two People**, followed in
1965. A married American businessman named
Forrest and an Italian boy named Marcello have a
love affair, but the city of Rome itself is a
more engaging character than either of Windham's
oddly matched protagonists. In his perceptive
assessment of the novel a few weeks in advance
of its publication, the Italian writer Mario
Soldati observed that the title was probably
untranslatable into Italian, since the book is
not about two lives but about two cultures or
two populaces in conflict. When the novel did
appear in Italian, **Due Vite** proved not entirely
accurate as a title; it is not so much a novel
about Forrest and Marcello as it is about the

cultures they represent. Windham supplies an
American sensibility through Forrest who seems
only slightly aware he has fallen into a
homosexual alliance without remarking its
absolute strangeness. Although he has evidence
through a married friend that such affairs are
not uncommon in Italy, he fails to register what
must have struck him as unexpected. Since the
novel passes entirely in Rome, Forrest -- as one
of the "two people" represented -- is at a
distinct disadvantage. Contrarily, Windham
creates a multi-faceted Italian sensibility
through Marcello's family life, as sweetly
painful as family life inevitably is, and in the
broader delineation of the city itself.

That Marcello and Forrest accept their
affair so easily turned at least two otherwise
reasonable American critics -- Eliot Fremont-
Smith and Stanley Kauffman -- to moral outrage.
Because Forrest seemed to be unaware of his
critics' morality, and at the same time unable
to control what they could only identify as lust
for his young lover, those same two critics
turned to sneering invective. A third one,
Martin Levin, merely made fun of any genuine
sexual affection between two men, and out on the
West Coast Robert J. Kaller, in the **Monterey
Peninsula Herald**, approached hysteria in his
review over "a serious social evil" guaranteed
to taint anybody who condoned it.

To sensitive readers, however, **Two People**
demonstrates how easily categories fail either
to justify or to explain our behavior, just as
Forrest observes a confusion of the seasons, of
heaven and earth, of good and evil, even if he
does not question his passion for Marcello.
Forrest must eventually evoke a memory of Thomas
Mann's Aschenbach in **Death in Venice**, lurking
madly in narrow streets in secret pursuit of
Tadzio. Forrest ferrets out his young lover at
the beach, unable to control himself from doing
so, and then hides in fear of being seen. It is
a powerful sequence, as upsetting as Aschenbach's own, because Forrest, like his model,
does not seem fully to grasp what has happened
to him. Marcello, on the other hand, is no
latter-day version of Mann's pre-pubescent
Tazio, but a lonely boy alienated from his
father. That the alliance is essentially phys-

ical gives the book a false patina dispelled only with a second reading. Unlike Aschenbach, Forrest is in the end objective about the affair, and what it has implied, when the relationship has grown into something more:

> Love's power is that it lets you exist outside your own body. Forrest had seen the awareness of this power raised to an almost unbearable degree in his wife when she looked at their small children. He had seen it in the children, too, long before they could have been aware of the mortal traps of their own bodies; they watched their mother leave them with the incredulity of people watching their own selves walking away from them. It is present in affection's most immaterial manifestations, in the knowledge that your thoughts contain another person, or that another person has you in his mind. Its biological end is the creation of a new body, and because of this it has been taught that the love between men should remain chaste. But life is not so clearly defined. Forrest had suffered less from an aberration of thought when he felt that a part of himself was leaving him each time with Marcello than he had suffered from a failure to accept what was happening. He accepted it now. But it did not make him chaste. He was glad when he realized that, despite the change in their relationship, and whether for money, or desire, or affection, Marcello had come to the apartment that day, as he had come in the past, with the specific intention of going to bed. . . . And although he had not given much subsequent thought to his drunken longing to be reincarnated as a Roman, he sensed that it was at least in part himself that he held in his arms that afternoon. (234-35)

As an American, Forrest can never truly get beneath the skin of the Italian temperament; he can adore it, though only superficially or temporarily, manifested either in Marcello or in Rome itself, admiring in infinitesimal detail the beauty of the object, boy or city. This is

neither immediately obvious nor explicitly
voiced through Forrest, although from the outset
of the novel he is aware that he is the visitor,
Marcello the host. But a minor epiphany occurs
when they say goodbye for the last time that is
sufficiently clear to both of them: "Marcello
shook the hand that Forrest held out. Then he
took the American by the shoulders and kissed
him on each cheek, as Italians do their close
friends and relatives" (252).

To a friend, Windham observed that he did
not object to being called homosexual, nor
object to calling himself homosexual, even if he
didn't think of himself as "homosexual," enclos-
ing the word in his own quotation marks:

> I don't consider this category any more
> real than any others. This isn't something
> I thought up for **Two People**: categories, as
> I pointed out in **Emblems of Conduct**, are
> for me conventions of time and place "as
> misleading as they are convenient" that
> permit us to discuss events too upsetting
> to examine individually. Homosexuality and
> heterosexuality are equally artificial
> categories. As to "normal," normal would
> be bi-sexual, except that "bi-sexual" is as
> artificial a category as the other two,
> necessitated by their artificiality. Love
> is <u>not</u> an artificial category -- but at
> the price that no one agrees on what the
> word means. I would say the same thing for
> friendship.

At least one critic perceived in **Two People**
what finally gives the novel its unassailable
integrity: "Mr. Windham deploys a fairly simple
Latinate vocabulary in sentences of an almost
baroque complexity," wrote Michael Ratcliffe in
London's **Sunday Times**, "the best of which is
precisely calculated as to the exact moral and
syntactical weight that each word has to bear."

None of this fiction sold particularly well
or drew a strong response from many reviewers.
A careful reading through the annotations in
Section E of this bibliography, detailing those
responses, gives some indication of the way in
which the unfulfilled anticipations of reviewers
can sometimes lead to their own disappointment.

With disturbing regularity, critics have been
wont to insist that Windham ought to be writing
a kind of book that he was by temperament and
inclination unprepared to write and uninterested
in writing.

Subsequently, when publishers proved indifferent, Sandy Campbell published the books himself, in a series of volumes prepared by the
Stamperia Valdonega in Verona, Italy, under the
supervision of Martino Mardersteig. In an age
of "perfect" bindings from which glued leaves
detach themselves with aplomb, Campbell's
splendid editions eradicate the distinction
between the bookmaker's craft and art. Four of
these books were picked up for popular editions
that proved sufficiently successful to warrant
subsequent paperback versions. But the kind of
attention Donald Windham's work deserves has
continued to elude him. It was a source of some
considerable satisfaction to Sandy Campbell, not
long before his death, that a trade edition from
a powerful American publisher of two of his
Italian publications, **As if . . .** and **Footnote
to a Friendship**, was issued as **Lost Friendships**
in 1987. He was prouder perhaps of his own
beautiful edition of Windham's memoir to accompany the letters of Alice B. Toklas to them,
issued that same year. Doubtless, he would have
been pleased that Windham continued these dis-
tinguished Stamperia Valdonega Editions with a
memorial volume of Campbell's own memoirs of
James Joyce's widow Nora, E. M. Forster, and
Alfred Lunt and Lynn Fontanne. The book will
prove to be valuable as resource material for
scholars as well as an aesthetic pleasure for
collectors, even if Campbell wasn't the writer
in the family.

He had published Windham's fourth novel a
decade earlier: **Tanaquil, or The Hardest Thing
of All**, its binding splendidly wrapped in a
signed and numbered lithograph by Tony Smith and
boxed in a bright yellow slipcase. The book is
a surprising departure from its predecessors; it
makes markedly different demands and offers
markedly different pleasures, a deliberately
old-fashioned love story, early nineteenth century in scope but mid-twentieth century in
attitude, heavily peopled with a supporting cast
of eccentrics. The form and content are not

entirely compatible because the leisurely pace
and sprawling plot are sometimes at odds with
each other, although admittedly readers' expec-
tations don't always coincide with a writer's
intentions. Several scenes in **Tanaquil** are only
summarized after the fact, but their implicit
drama might have enriched the time-marking
familiar enough in, say, Richardson or Dickens
or Trollope. Conversely, some scenes and events
go nowhere after they have begun, becoming
instead a series of dramatized cul-de-sacs, as
if Windham wanted to fix in fiction some momen-
tary circumstance of private meaning. Art may
imitate life, and perhaps it must, but the
essential aimlessness of reality demands some
transformation for the reader who may not have
shared it with the writer. **Tanaquil** is Windham's most conventional novel, a long series of
incidents interlocking the lives of many characters, with a happy ending for the eponymous
heroine and her husband, Frankie. "Attractive"
and "attracted to" may appear more often than
any other adjective and verb in the book, aside
from the names of the leading characters; people
are almost resolutely "attracted to" and
"attractive" to others, especially Frankie. But
like his all too attractive Byronic counter-
parts, Richardson's Lovelace or Austen's Darcy,
he is seductive, self-centered, and jealous,
easily lured into infidelities and fully capable
of initiating some of his own; so the depression
that overtakes him late in the novel does not
easily arouse compassion. There is not a great
deal in his character or behavior to inspire
Tanaquil's loyalty and devotion other than his
surpassing good looks. When late in the novel
Frankie observes that he is getting fat around
the middle, he has good reason to worry because
he has little going for him but his physical
beauty. He is essentially ingenuous, although
that hardly justifies his sometimes errant
heart. As in many novels in the genre from
which this one grows, however, he and Tanaquil
are show-cased against a remarkable range of
richly inventive characters: Page, who is George
Platt Lynes; Dickinson, who is Joseph Cornell;
Stepa, who is Pavel Tchelitchew; the haunted,
alcoholic Jeanne; a sailor astonishingly tat-
tooed; Patricia, masking her vulnerability with

predatory aplomb. They are all individualized,
engaging, memorable. So to a lesser degree are
the representatives of a pontificating older
generation; so are Frankie's and Tanaquil's
children, Joy and Sandy. Eventually the novel
appeared in both hardback and paperback trade
editions, lightly revised and without its sub-
title, but reviewers were indifferent and sales
were modest.

Windham's most recent novel, published only
in Campbell's limited edition, printed at the
Stamperia Valdonega and therefore little known
in America, is a wildly intricate adventure:
Stone in the Hourglass. Dealing with corruption
in the arts -- both painting and literature --
it is an unequivocal, intellectual tour de force
pretending to be an thriller. Some larcenous
portraits of actual people populate this book,
notably Truman Capote, and Windham has never
before demonstrated such a wicked sense of
humor. An intellectual mayhem pervades every
preposterous turn of the plot, ominously abetted
by false clues, red herrings, even murder, and a
good deal of suspense on at least two occasions;
but mysteries are supposed to end with villains
revealed, and with virtue, if not rewarded, once
again possible. Windham's purposes here are
darker: Corruption in the arts is as subversive
as in any other field, and the innocent suffer
long before and long after the guilty. **Stone in
the Hourglass** is operatic, but the impediments
that disrupt time to give the plot its bewilder-
ingly elaborate twists -- the hourglass that,
turned, measures both fame and failure -- are
toughly grounded in the same "reality" that
informs and often afflicts everything Windham
has written, even in the disguise of a witty
thriller like **Stone in the Hourglass.**

Any assessment of any writer's work ought
to demand that its faults be acknowledged;
Donald Windham has his fair share, clearly
enough. Readers eager to turn pages swiftly
should look elsewhere because the narrative
drive in Windham's work is not encouraged by a
dramatic one; it is difficult to imagine films
or television mini-series being made from many
of his novels or stories because they are too
interior, although he dramatized "The Starless
Air" himself and it was produced with some

success. His characters are often ordinary
enough to be unengaging, despite notable exceptions, like William Dickinson, the unforgettable
Joseph Cornell figure in **Tanaquil**, for example,
and the hilariously evil Dietrich de Graab and
nasty Digby Jones in **Stone in the Hourglass**.
Usually, however, there are no heroes or villains, and rarely are there the kinds of memorable oddballs whose appearance in most fiction
seems inevitable. Windham's women are often
undefined, their actions insufficiently
motivated. Characters both male and female are
often too easily prey to human frailty to be
entirely likeable, which may of course be only
another way of saying they are too real.
Blackie Pride, for instance, the unrepentant
juvenile delinquent in **The Dog Star**, asks no
quarter and Windham gives him even less; protagonist and antagonist are terms that cannot
apply because the boy is both and neither, and
the reader is likely to admire him only grudg-
ingly. Denis Freeman in **The Hero Continues** is
fully capable of using others and of being used,
sometimes in genuinely ugly ways, and to become
a <u>free man</u> he must become free <u>of</u> men; the line
between is indiscernible and therefore uncom-
fortably familiar. These reservations hold in
Windham's later fiction as well. Despite the
loneliness that brings them together, the
middle-aged American in **Two People** is so accept-
ing of the affair that he sometimes seems astonishingly imperceptive, and his young lover's
attitude comes off as mere diffidence, which may
be accurate in life but proves unnerving in art.
Tanaquil and Frankie occupy similar positions,
although Windham's New York in **Tanaquil** --
richly enough evoked -- does not approach his
Rome in **Two People**. Finally, his overarching
honesty and clarity can become their own adver-
saries, since readers demand that fiction offer
the disguise of reality rather than reality
itself. Art, after all, shares its root with
artifice.
     None of these reservations, however,
carries much weight against the strength of a
painter's eye for detail and a lapidary's care
for language. In Windham's nonfiction, his
faults -- if indeed they are faults in the last
analysis -- even serve as additional virtues on

occasion. As editor of Sandy Campbell's memoirs
of Forster, Joyce's widow Nora, and Lunt and
Fontanne, and of the letters to Campbell and to
himself, Windham has proven himself well nigh
faultless, although Campbell deserves substantial credit for the labor that went into
these volumes. Windham's introductions, running
commentaries, and notes are not only valuable
for biographers of these figures but pleasurable
to read for their clarity and warmth. **Tennessee
Williams' Letters to Donald Windham 1940-65**,
however, first published privately with Williams's
written permission in one of Campbell's limited
editions and then issued in both hardcover and
paperback trade editions, motivated an incred-
ible series of accusations against Windham in
reviews, resulting in his extraordinary lawsuit
over libel. The story is all spelled out in
several of the entries in this bibliography.
Unfortunately, the attendant publicity over-
shadowed Windham's achievement; his work is a
model of scholarly patience.

Similarly, but for different reasons,
Emblems of Conduct and **Lost Friendships** are
equally superb, carefully observed, with quiet
humor or pathos or both, and an unfailing
compassion and objectivity toward their subjects. Inevitably, passages out of context do
not begin to represent a writer's own peculiar
magic, but something of "A Coin with a Hole in
It" from **Emblems of Conduct** may be sufficiently
suggestive.

In this brief chapter, a young vagrant cuts
up some kindling for nine- or ten-year-old Donald's mother and aunt, in exchange for something to eat. The woodpile itself, "accumulated
from the collapse of a number of buildings,"
seems to speak for the slow decay of the homeplace of "The Starless Air" in **The Warm Country**,
that late-Victorian house where Windham grew up
fatherless with his mother and brother and an
aunt and her children:

> First the doghouse and the fence around the
> dog yard had been pulled down. Then the
> chicken house. Finally, part of the barn.
> None of these had been demolished deliber-
> ately; they had simply sagged toward the
> earth until my brother and I, or our cous-

ins, knocked them over in play, and the
loose boards had been cleaned up and moved
to this spot. . . . (54)

Donald falls into conversation with the young
stranger, who talks about his own childhood, his
family, the sea, remote lands with strange names
where he has travelled, and Donald in turn
shares his limited horizon: the house, the
yard, a trip to Florida when he was so young he
does not remember it but for having been told he
was there. The intimacy makes him feel as he
did "when the rain or the night changed the
familiar landscape of the back yard into a place
as different from its usual self as a foreign
city would be -- an alien feeling that seemed in
some odd way to connect me to the stranger"
(58). Together they stack the kindling; then
before he leaves he gives Donald a Chinese coin
-- valueless he admits -- to remember him by.
Windham's elegaic conclusion, free of any sentimental plea, is nevertheless heartbreaking, in
uncommon language sculpted into our common
anguish:

> When I looked at the copper-colored coin, I
> thought of the vagrant's brown plaid shirt;
> of how, on the inside, where the sleeve was
> rolled up, I had seen the plaid pattern
> repeated in a lighter tan the same shade as
> his face, as though the sun at the same
> time that it had faded his shirt had dark-
> ened his skin until the two met. The color
> joined with the brown fading snap-shots of
> my father in our family photograph album,
> snapshots of places as flat and strange as
> the foreign names the stranger had used --
> stretches of sand at Daytona Beach, or
> level fields in pine wood cleared for grow-
> ing pineapples. Between the shirt and the
> photographs there was the copper-colored
> coin in my hand. And somehow, out of the
> combination of all three, emerged the exact
> shade of my own longing and belief. (60)

Writing of the work of the Italian Renaissance painter Sandro Botticelli, Walter Pater
rightly observed that "besides those great men,"
there were others who had "a peculiar quality of

pleasure that we cannot get elsewhere" who
deserved attention from those who had "felt
their charm strongly," often with "a special
diligence and a consideration wholly affectionate, just because there is not about them the
stress of a great name and authority" (50). He
might well have been referring to writers who
have never been given their fair share of attention, either from popular readers or from
academics, Donald Windham among them.

When **The Dog Star** was published at the
beginning of Windham's career, Thomas Mann
called it "a good, sincere, and highly gifted
piece of work" because it was "simple, natural,
and strong." The observation is applicable to
nearly everything that followed.

"Footnote from a Would-be
Lop-eared Rabbit"
by Donald Windham

One characteristic of a bibliography
is that it does not tell where a writer's work
was not published. And that can be a part of
his publishing history, even if a part that
looms larger for the writer than for his
reader.
Toward the end of **The Way of All Flesh**,
the protagonist, Ernest Pontifex, begins his
career as an author. Since his being an author
has no real pertinence to the main theme of the
novel, I suspect that Samuel Butler used this
device to express his own publishing history
that no bibliography would reflect. Pontifex
is protecting his discovery of how unmarketable
his work is. Everything he writes is rejected.
He puts it this way:

> Why, if I was a well-bred horse, or
> sheep, or a pure-bred pigeon or lop-
> eared rabbit I would be more saleable.
> If I was even a cathedral in a colonial
> town people would give me something,
> but as it is they do not want me.
> (363-64)

From the beginning, this was the case with
me and United States publishers and editors.
One might assume from a bibliography that I was
a wider traveler in my youth than was Tennessee
Williams, who was continually criss-crossing the
United States. My first published story

appeared in **Sur**, Victoria Ocampo's Argentine
literary magazine, in 1943, the next in Cyril
Connolly's British **Horizon** in 1947. But far
from being in Buenos Aires or London, I was in
New York in these years, submitting my stories
one after the other to the U. S. magazines I
hoped would print them.

In 1943, a prose poem of mine was published in Charles Henri Ford's surrealist
magazine, **View**. It appeared on the "Children's
Page," side by side with prose poems by "S. B.,
a female Mongolian-Idiot, aged 23." And
that was where most U. S. fiction editors
seemed to consider that I belonged, rather
than with their pure-bred pigeons and lop-
eared rabbits.

I had first submitted "The Warm Country,"
the story that Cyril Connolly accepted for
Horizon, in this country to **Story** magazine
at the end of 1941, accompanied by a letter from
Tennessee Williams recommending it to Whit
Burnett, the editor, who had published
Tennessee's first mature story two years
earlier. After its rejection by **Story**, both
before and after its appearance in **Horizon**, "The
Warm Country" was submitted to and <u>not</u> published
by **Atlantic Monthly**, **Esquire**, **Harper's**, **Harper's
Bazaar**, **Mademoiselle**, **Partisan Review**, and almost
every other U. S. magazine that printed serious
fiction. It first appeared here in the book of
stories to which it gave its name, in 1962 --
two years following the book's publication in
England.

Ten years after I started trying, in 1952,
I at last sold a story to a national U. S.
magazine. The magazine was **Mademoiselle**. The
story was "The New Moon with the Old Moon in Her
Arms." I had sent the story to the magazine
over a year earlier. The fiction editor had
rejected it as "not up to your usual high standing," a pretty thorough spurning, as she had
rejected every story I had previously sent her.
Then it was published in England in **The
Listener**, of which J. R. Ackerley was literary
editor. The editor-in-chief of **Mademoiselle**
read it there, took it to the fiction editor
and said, in effect: "This is the kind of story
we want for **Mademoiselle**; see if you can get the
American rights."

And so I joined the pure-bred pigeons and lop-eared rabbits -- but only briefly.

"The Starless Air," written at the same time as "The New Moon With the Old Moon in Her Arms," was turned down by **Atlantic Monthly, Esquire, Harper's, Harper's Bazaar**, and **Partisan Review**; also by **The New Yorker, Furioso, Tomorrow, Hudson Review, Sewanee Review, Yale Review**, the **Virginia Quarterly**; and, when my first novel, **The Dog Star**, was published by Doubleday and an enthusiastic promotion man there sent the story where he believed he could get it published, by **Good Housekeeping, Cosmopolitan**, and **Today's Woman**.

Another ten years after my appearance in **Mademoiselle**, when my collection of stories came out, only one more of them had been published in a U. S. magazine, although most of them had appeared elsewhere.

The one other story was "The Third Bridge" in **Noonday**. The editor wanted Noonday Press to bring out a collection of my short fiction. It was he who suggested that I ask E. M. Forster to write a blurb for the jacket. Forster replied by offering to write an introduction. Despite Forster's introduction, the sales department, or in any case someone beyond the editor of **Noonday**, scotched the project for the book. So Forster wrote to the head editor at Harcourt, Brace & Co., his publisher in the U. S., and recommended the collection to him. And the editor asked to see the manuscript. And I submitted it to him. And he turned it down too. And so I was also not published by Noonday Press and Harcourt, Brace & Co.

I had better not go into the history of the book publishers who did not publish me. It looms too large. I'll just say that, looking back, I believe almost everything that has happened to me in my life has, in the long run, been for the best. Including those twenty years of U. S. magazines' rejections of my short stories. I understand their reasons for this no more now than I did while it was happening. Book publishers have their sales departments. Increasingly, they submit manuscripts to them for final decisions. But magazines? About short stories?

Anyway, perhaps it is best not to be a

lop-eared rabbit. I have a postcard I bought
in France of a dog wearing paper rabbit ears.
He looks happy. But the caption reads: <u>Le</u>
<u>bonnet d'ane.</u>*

----
* Whether one translates this "donkey's bonnet"
  as a Shakespearean "Ass's Head," or simpler
  "Fool's Cap," the fact remains: the dog looks
  as happy as a best-selling author.

Works Cited in Introduction and Footnote:

Butler, Samuel. **The Way of All Flesh**, Shrewsbury
    Edition, Henry Festing Jones and A. B. Bar-
    tholomew, Editors, volume 17. New York: AMS
    Press, reprint edition, 1968.
Ferro, Robert. "Between the Covers," **Gay News**,
    4-10 February 1983.
Forster, E. M. "Introduction," **The Warm Country**
    by Donald Windham. London: Rupert Hart-
    Davis, 1960.
Kaller, Robert J. "Argument for Evil," **Monterey
    Peninsula Herald**, 19 September 1965.
Mann, Thomas. quoted in "Thomas Mann Sees Need
    for Anti-Fascism, **New York Herald Tribune**,
    29 April 1950.
Pater, Walter. **The Renaissance**. New York: The
    Modern Library, n.d.
Ratcliffe, Michael, "Current Fiction," [London]
    Sunday Times, 13 February 1966.
Van Vechten, Carl. **Excavations**. New York: Knopf,
    1926.
Windham, Donald. **Emblems of Conduct**. New York:
    Scribners, 1963.
---. **Two People**. New York: Coward-McCann, 1965.
---. **The Warm Country**. London: Rupert Hart-
    Davis, 1960.

Editorial Note

Bibliographers gratefully pillage the work
of Donald Gallup, whose Ezra Pound and T. S.
Eliot bibliographies have established precedents
of inarguable excellence, and I welcome the
opportunity to say so. With minor variations, I
have followed his models. Each entry lists editions of a volume in chronological order of
publication, regardless of the language or country of origin in which it first appeared. I
have cross-referenced reprintings by including
in brackets at the conclusion of the entries my
corresponding numbers. My descriptive phrase-
ology is conventional whenever possible, and I
have avoided specifying outre variations in
color. Edges are unstained and endpapers are
white unless otherwise specified. In transcrib-
ing title pages and colophons I have indicated
italics by underlining; otherwise, titles are in
bold-face. Missing information from an entry
was unavailable. I have given full attention to
bindings and packaging, particularly for the
Stamperia Valdonega Editions, including a full
accounting for line divisions in colophons and
epigraphs since Mardersteig insisted on their
looking correct to him, even if that entailed
rewording at his request. Also, Windham and
Campbell were intimately involved in the design
of these books.
    Section A contains all books and pamphlets
in all editions, printings, states, and trans-
lations, the contents of which are solely

Windham's work.

Section B contains books and pamphlets for which Windham served as editor or for which he prepared prefaces or introductions, as well as those prepared by others to which he contributed or in which his work appeared.

Section C contains periodical writings.

Section D contains ephemera, some of which might qualify for listing elsewhere in another bibliographer's opinion. In most instances, however, the material in this section was not only printed as ephemera -- dust jacket blurbs, short program notes, endorsements for work by others -- but written as ephemera.

Section E accounts for biographical and critical studies or listings, interviews, and references to Windham's work in studies of other artists and writers; further, it includes a selective representation of reviews of Windham's books, but deliberately I have ignored insignificant notices or those that fail to illuminate either his virtues or shortcomings as a writer. I have quoted from these without comment, or I have paraphrased them depending on the content, or I have combined quotation and paraphrase, and when appropriate I have commented on them. Even a cursory perusal will indicate the wide divergence of opinion about Windham's work and how superficial some reviewers may be in assessing books, larding their observations with quips rather than close assessments -- positive or negative -- of the work under consideration. Equally telling, many of them demonstrate the kind of hostility that many good writers have endured because of their subject matter. The number of reviews I have allotted one book does not therefore always equal the number I have allotted another one.

The index lists major titles by Windham and titles with which he was associated. It lists names of all individuals as subjects and the names of all significant individuals as authors. It does not list the names of minor reviewers peripherally connected with Windham's career.

For the foregoing divisions and decisions, and for errors and omissions, I assume responsibility, defending the former and apologizing -- especially to the subject -- for the latter.

DONALD WINDHAM

A. Books and Pamphlets

A 1   YOU TOUCHED ME!   **1947**

a.   First edition

<u>You Touched Me!</u> / A ROMANTIC COMEDY / IN THREE
ACTS / <u>by Tennessee Williams</u> / <u>and Donald
Windham</u> / Suggested by a short story of the same
/ name by D. H. Lawrence / [publisher's device]
/ <u>SAMUEL FRENCH</u> / PRICE 75 CENTS [all of the
foregoing in descending lines] / 25 West 45th
St. NEW YORK / 811 West 7th St. LOS ANGELES /
<u>LONDON</u> . <u>TORONTO</u>

137 pp., 19.3 X 13.1 cm., all edges trimmed.

[1] half-title; [2] blank; [3] title; [4]
copyrights, 1922, 1942, 1947; [5] first cast
list; [6] breakdown of scenes; [7] Act One; [8]-
114, text; 115-[137] plot, props, character
list, lights, setting. A photograph of the set
is tipped-in between [2] and [3].

Green cloth boards, title and authors printed on
spine and front in gold. Green and white dust
jacket with photograph of Edmund Gwenn, Cather-
ine Willard, and Montgomery Clift on front;
advertisements on back; plot summary on front
flap.

506 copies published 1947. $2.00.

b.   Paperback edition, issued simultaneously

Identical to A1a, with the following exceptions:
Stiff cream (on advance copies) or gray paper
wrappers printed in black, duplicating title
page; back and inside covers list other plays.
A second printing, otherwise unidentified, was
bound in orange wrappers. 18.7 X 13.1 cm.

500 copies published 1947. $.75 for advance
copies; raised to $.85 for subsequent copies and
printings.

> In 1942, Windham conceived of the idea
> of a play based on Lawrence's short
> story and had nearly completed a first
> draft when Tennessee Williams suggested
> that they collaborate on the dramatiza-
> tion. It was copyrighted that year as
> an unpublished play and given its first
> performance at the Cleveland Play House
> in October 1943. The following month,
> it was produced at the Pasadena Play-
> house in California, prior to which
> Windham persuaded Williams to make some
> cuts. The play opened on Broadway in
> October 1945, produced by Guthrie
> McClintic. Neither the Lawrence story,
> nor the Williams-Windham script, nor the
> Cleveland and Pasadena productions,
> contains an exclamation mark in the
> title. This was added by the McClintic
> office for the Broadway production and
> subsequently appeared in all printed
> versions.

A 2   THE DOG STAR   **1950**

a.   First edition

BY DONALD WINDHAM THE / DOG STAR [author's name
in smaller typeface] / DOUBLEDAY & COMPANY,
INC., GARDEN CITY, NEW YORK, 1950

i-ii+221 pp., 19. x 13. cm., top edges trimmed,
fore-edges rough trimmed.

[i-ii] blank; [1] title; [2] disavowal of actual

characters and events portrayed and copyright;
[3] dedication: To Fred Melton; [4] blank; [5]
half-title; [6] blank; 7-221, text.

Medium blue cloth printed down spine in silver
to imitate author and title from title page.
Matching blue dust jacket with a lithographic
illustration by D. Reynolds printed in black
with title in pumpkin and highlights on the
figure of a boy and "A NOVEL" in white; photograph by Sandy Campbell of Windham in the Villa
Borghese, Rome, and biography on back; blurb by
Tennessee Williams above blue rectangle on front
flap; plot summary on back flap.

Published 20 April 1950. $2.50.

> Begun in 1942 and rewritten many times,
> **The Dog Star** was based on the life of
> Fred Melton's brother. Although it was
> praised by Thomas Mann and E. M. Fors-
> ter, it did not sell well. A month in
> advance of publication, Windham signed
> four or five hundred sheets to be
> tipped-in for sale in Atlanta, Georgia,
> where he had been born. Six months
> after publication, on 16 October 1950,
> 1900 copies of **The Dog Star** were
> remaindered in the original binding and
> jacket.

b.   First paperback edition

THE / DOG STAR / by / Donald Windham /
[publisher's logo] / SIGNET BOOK / Published by
 THE NEW AMERICAN LIBRARY

144 pp., 17.7 X 10.8 cm. all edges trimmed and
stained red.

[1] plot summary and review squibs; [2] advertisements for other Signet books; [3] title; [4]
copyright 1950, first printing April 1951; [5]
To Fred Melton; [6] blank; [7]-144, text.

Full color stiff paper wrappers, publisher's
logo, number 871, and "A compelling story of
love and violence" at top; title in yellow,
author in white, printed over an illustration of

a boy with a guitar and a girl on a bed with a
comic book; "A SIGNET BOOK" and "Complete and
Unabridged" at bottom; biographical squib, small
uncredited photograph of Windham by Fred Melton;
passage from the novel and blurb by Tennessee
Williams on back.

Published April 1951. $.25.

c.   First English edition

THE / DOG STAR / A NOVEL BY / DONALD WINDHAM /
[STAR] / [publisher's logo] / LONDON / RUPERT
HART-DAVIS / 1951

240 pp., 2.4 X 14.0 cm., all edges trimmed.

[1-2] blank; [3] half-title; [4] blank; [5]
title; [6] dedication / printed in France / by
Regie le Livre Universel. / 7-[240] text.

Red cloth printed across spine in silver, title,
star, author, publisher. Light blue, white,
brown, and red dust jacket with illustration of
a boy smoking at a window and a girl on a bed
behind him, designed by Charles Mozley; publisher's name on back flap; plot summary and
blurb by Thomas Mann on front flap.

Published 14 September 1951. 12/6.

d.   French edition

DU MONDE ENTRIER [printed in a semi-circle] /
DONALD WINDHAM / canicule / (THE DOG STAR) /
traduit de l'americain par / ELISABETH VAN
RYSSELBERGHE / roman / [publisher's logo] / nrf
/ GALLIMARD

240 pp., 18.7 X 11.7 cm., all edges unopened and
untrimmed.

[1-2] blank; [3] half-title; [4] blank; [5]
title; [6] limitation note: 6o numbered copies
and six copies lettered A through F on velin pur
fil Lafuma Navarre; 7-238, text, [239] ACHÈVE
D'IMPRIMER EN DECEMBRE 1954 PAR EMMANUEL GREVIN
ET FILS A LAGNY-SUR-MARNE.

Stiff ivory paper wrappers printed in black to
duplicate title page but with title and nrf
printed in red on front, plot summary, and
author's biography, comparing his writing to
Andre Gide's on back.

Published December 1954.   500fr.

e.   Limited French edition

Identical with A2f, with the following exceptions: 18.8 X 12.0 cm.; copies numbered and
lettered as indicated in the limitation note;
pale lime paper wrapper under a glassine
wrapper; list of publisher's other books in
place of assessment.

f.   Second paperback edition, bowdlerized

LET ME / ALONE / [THE DOG STAR] / A NOVEL OF
YOUTH IN TORMENT / DONALD WINDHAM / POPULAR
LIBRARY . NEW YORK

144 pp., 17.5 X 10.8 cm., all edges trimmed and
stained green.

[1] advertisement and note about the author; [2]
review squibs; [3] title; [4] June 1956, list of
publisher's titles, dedication; 5-144, text.

Full color stiff paper wrappers, publisher's
logo, number 754, and "A Tough Teen-Ager in
Search of Manhood" at top; title in red, illustration of a boy with a knife and a sexy girl in
the background; advertisement quotation and a
second illustration, this time of the boy
embracing the girl, on back cover.

Published June 1956. $.25.

> Although advertised on the cover as
> "Complete and unabridged," this edition
> of **The Dog Star** was expurgated through-
> out: "contraceptives," p. 9; "put lead
> in your pencil," p. 14; "Remember that
> when your pecker gets hard," p. 66;
> "pricks" altered to "bastards," p. 69;
> "hair curled pubes," p. 108; "there,
> just once," p. 115.   The title was

changed without Windham's permission or knowledge.

g.   English paperback edition

LET ME ALONE / DONALD WINDHAM / THE HARBOROUGH PUBLISHING CO., LTD., / 44 E. BEDFORD ROAD, LONDON W.C. 11

156 pp., 17.7 X 11.1 cm., all edges trimmed.

[1] half-title; [2] advertisements for James Baldwin's books; [3] title; [4] "Bound edition published in England in 1951 under The Dog Star," copyrights 1950 and 1959, dedication; 5-156, text; [157-60] advertisements for ACE Books.

Stiff paper wrapppers with an illustration based on the American version; blurbs by publisher and Thomas Mann on back cover.

Published 1959. 2/6.

The edition reprinted the original text although it used the title of the bowd-lerized edition.

A 3   THE HITCHHIKER   **1950**

a.   First edition

THE HITCHHIKER / BY / DONALD WINDHAM

16 pp., 26.1 X 18.5 cm., all edges trimmed.

[1-2] blank; [3] title; [4] blank; 5-13, text;[14] blank; [15] <u>This edition of The Hitchhiker is limited to 250 copies, each copy signed by the author, printed in Florence, Italy, in August, 1950, by the Tipografia Giuntina. This is No:</u>

Buff paper wrapper, with title and author in orange printed on the front, duplicating [minus "by"] the title page; ivory text stock stapled into wrapper.

250 copies issued 4 August 1950. $2.50.

b.   Reserved edition

Copies 1-5 of A3a were bound in tan leather
boards with title and author printed in gold on
the front, none for sale.

> **The Hitchhiker** was the first of Sandy
> Campbell's publications, issued when
> Windham had had no success in selling
> his stories to magazines. He had it
> printed at the Tipografia Guintina in
> Florence, a commercial business firm
> that had printed G. Orioli's handsome
> Lungarno series of the work of D. H.
> Lawrence and Norman Douglas, writers
> whose works both Campbell and Windham
> admired. To get **The Hitchhiker** to
> America without running the risk of
> losing all of the copies at once through
> the difficulties of the Italian postal
> system, Campbell and Windham mailed
> them in bundles of 25 copies each to
> various friends in New York. The story
> was reprinted in **Christopher Street**
> [C59].

A 4   **SERVANTS WITH TORCHES**   **1950**

SERVANTS WITH TORCHES / Donald Windham [the
foregoing in black across a line drawing by
Bernard Perlin in pale orange of a carabiniere's
insignia, resembling a flaming urn]

viii+28 pp., 18.0 X 26.0 cm., all edges
untrimmed.

[i] blank; [ii] portrait of an Italian carabiniere in rust, cream, dark brown, and grey-
blue on a tipped-in brown leaf, by Paul Cadmus,
numbered and signed by the artist; [iii] half-
title printed in brown to fill the entire page:
SERVANT / S WITH / TORCHES; [iv-vi] blank; [vii]
title; [viii] blank; 1-24, text; [25-26] blank;
[27] This edition of SERVANTS WITH TORCHES, /
printed in New York City, in February 1955, /
consists of 117 copies. Four copies are

lettered / A, B, C, D; thirteen copies are
numbered I-XIII; / one hundred copies are
numbered 1-100. The / silk screen illustration
by Paul Cadmus is done / especially for the
edition, and is numbered and / signed by the
artist. All copies are signed by / the author.
/ This is copy No. [the foregoing printed over
a smaller version of the insignia on the title
page]

Black paper boards with pale orange carbiniere's
insignia on front; black endpapers; black dust
jacket printed in pale orange to duplicate half-
title.

117 copies issued February 1955. $8.00.

> Originally, Fred Melton had planned to
> silk-screen **Servants With Torches**
> entirely in Windham's own holograph;
> eventually, however, Melton's Pippin
> Press silk-screened only the dust
> jacket, cover, half-title, title, and
> insignia under type on the colophon
> page. There were ten additional copies
> as artist's proofs of the Cadmus
> frontispiece. A number of copies of the
> book were damaged by water, of which
> eighteen were subsequently destroyed.
> **Servants With Torches** was collected in
> **The Warm Country** [A7].

A 5   THE KELLY BOYS   **1957**

Atlanta May, 1939 / When I leave this town I
shall miss the Kelly boys. . . .

4 pp., 16.5 X 12.5 cm., untrimmed.

[1-3] text, continuing after the sentence above;
[4] 240 COPIES OF "THE KELLY BOYS" HAVE BEEN /
PRINTED IN NEW YORK CITY IN JANUARY, 1957. /
THIS IS COPY NUMBER [number in orange ink]

Single tan leaf printed in rust, French-folded
to make four pages, enclosed in a matching
envelope with THE KELLY BOYS printed in the
upper left-hand corner, designed by Sandy Camp-

bell and printed by a job printer.

240 copies issued January 1957, none for sale.

> **The Kelly Boys** appears in **Emblems of Conduct** [A8], pp. 164-66, where it is introduced as the earliest piece of writing that Windham ever conserved.

A 6   THE HERO CONTINUES   **1960**

a.   First edition

Donald Windham / [line] / THE HERO / CONTINUES / [publisher's logo] / Rupert Hart-DAVIS / SOHO SQUARE LONDON / 1960

192 pp., 19.7 X 13.1 cm., all edges trimmed.

[1] half-title; [2] by the same author, / the dog star; [3] title; [4] copyright Donald Windham 1960, printed in Great Britain; [5] dedication: To Tennessee Williams; [6] blank; 7-191, text; [192] blank.

Pebbled green cloth, author, title, and publisher printed across spine in silver. Black, red, and cream dust jacket with illustration by Heather Standring of a man in an overcoat standing on the pavement on front, title and full back in red; publisher's address on back flap; plot summary on front flap.

Published 1 May 1960. 15/-.

b.   First American edition

Donald Windham / [line] / THE HERO / CONTINUES / A NOVEL / THOMAS Y. CROWELL COMPANY / NEW YORK ESTABLISHED 1834

192 pp., 20.2 X 13.5 cm., all edges trimmed.

[1] half-title; [2] By the same author / THE DOG STAR; [3] title; [4] Copyright 1960 by Donald Windham, rights statement; Printed in the United States of America, Library of Congress Card No. 60-12542; [5] dedication; [6] blank; 7-191,

text; [192] blank.

Medium blue cloth boards, author's last name
across, title down, and publisher's last name
across spine printed in white; blue, black, and
white dust jacket, on front with author and
title: "A Novel of the Theatre"; on back, photograph by Sandy Campbell of Windham on the steps
to the Bethesda Fountain in Central Park, and a
biographical note.

Published 12 August 1960. $3.50.

> Printed by photo-offset from the English
> edition, the American edition carried a
> few corrections, none of them substan-
> tive: p. 43, "it" altered to "I"; p.
> 73, "la" to "le"; p. 127, "any grant" to
> "for any grant"; p. 178, question mark
> added.

c.   English paperback edition

The Hero Continues / Donald Windham / [pub-
lisher's logo] / FOUR SQUARE BOOKS

[1] half-title; [2] blank; [3] title; [4]
dedication, copyright 1960, first published in
Great Britain 1960, Four Square Edition 1966; 5-
[158] text; [159] publisher's advertisement;
[160] blank.

160 pp., 18.1 X 10.8 cm., all edges trimmed.

Stiff paper wrappers, illustration of a man on
the front printed in black, white, orange, yellow, and peach; "The stark, revealing story of a
man's fight against the corruption of success";
similar illustration on the back with plot
blurb.

Published 1966.   15/-.

A 7   THE WARM COUNTRY   **1960**

a.   First edition

THE WARM COUNTRY / DONALD WINDHAM / with an

introduction by E. M. FORSTER / [publisher's logo] / RUPERT HART-DAVIS / SOHO SQUARE LONDON / 1960

208 pp., 19.6 X 13 cm., all edges trimmed.

[1] half-title; [2] By the same author / THE DOG STAR / THE HERO CONTINUES; [3] title; [4] copyright Donald Windham, printed in Great Britain by Charles Birchall & Sons, Ltd., Liverpool and London; [5] dedication: to Paul Cadmus; [6] blank; [7] table of contents; [8] blank; [9-10] Introduction; 11-208, text.

Contents: Rosebud, 11 [C17]; The Seventh Day, 33 [C3]; The Starless Air, 43 [B3]; Servants with Torches, 75 [A4]; New Dominoes, 91; Flesh Farewell, 99 [B1]; The New Moon with the Old Moon in Her Arms, 109 [C18, C20]; The Warm Country, 119 [C14, C38]; The Third Bridge, 133 [C30]; An Island of Fire, 147 [C19]; Paolo, 163 [B4, C27, C37]; Single Harvest, 175 [C16]; Life of Georgia, 193; Night, 207 [C5].

Burnt sienna cloth boards, with title, author, and publisher printed across spine in silver. Black, white, and orange dust jacket with an illustration by Heather Standring of a black man and a white man in front of a stylized brick wall; orange back with review blurbs for **The Hero Continues**; back flap blank; publisher's blurb on front flap.

3500 copies published 5 December 1960.   15/-.

b.   First American edition

DONALD WINDHAM / [swelled rule] / THE WARM / COUNTRY / [swelled rule] / With an introduction / by E. M. Forster / CHARLES SCRIBNER'S SONS / [swelled rule] / NEW YORK

208 pp., 20.3 X 13.6 cm., all edges trimmed.

[1] half-title; [2] By Donald Windham [three titles]; [3] title; [4] copyright and credits; [5] dedication; [6] blank; [7] table of contents; [8] blank; [9-10] introduction by E. M. Forster; 11-208, text. Contents as in A7a.

Orange cloth boards, author and title printed in black down spine. Black and white photographic enlargement of tweed pattern dust jacket lettered in yellow and white: photograph by Sandy Campbell, uncredited, of Windham by a poster for Verdi's **Otello** in Venice and biography on back; English reviews on back flap; plot blurb on front flap.

1500 copies published 11 April 1962. $3.50.

> The copyright page of Scribner's edition of **The Warm Country** [4] reads: "The stories in this collection first appeared in the following magazines: Botteghe Oscure, Horizon, The Listener, View and in the following anthologies: New Directions 10, copyright 1948 by New Directions; Noonday, No. 3, Copyright 1960 by Noonday Press, Inc. See contradictory note, B3.

c.   Paperback edition

Identical to A7b, with the following exceptions: Bright pink, black, and white stiff paper wrappers, "Scribner's First Editions" and publisher's logo on front; on back, notice of two other books in the series: **The Butterfly** by Michael Rumaker and **For Love, Poems 1950-1960** by Robert Creely, cropped version of A7b dust jacket photograph and biographical note. 20.3 X 13.5 cm.

5000 copies published 11 April 1962. $1.65.

> The English edition preceded the American edition by two years; the American edition was made by photo-offset. Sales of the bound edition soon exceeded the 1500 copies available; by 30 August 1962, Scribner's had sold 1708 bound copies, some presumably from the paperback edition.

A 8   EMBLEMS OF CONDUCT   1964

a.   First edition

[woodcut in green of large wooden house based on a photograph of Windham's Atlanta home, by W. Ferro] / EMBLEMS OF CONDUCT / by Donald Windham / CHARLES SCRIBNER'S SONS, New York

[i] blank; [ii] BY DONALD WINDHAM [four titles]; [iii] half-title; [iv] first epigraph / [v] title; [vi] copyright and reprint acknowledgments; [vii] dedication: To Sandy Campbell; [viii] blank; [ix] second epigraph; [x] blank; [xi] contents; [xii] blank; 1-210, text; [211-12] blank.

212 pp., 21.5 X 15.2 cm., all edges trimmed.

Contents: The Dark Night, 1; The Man Who Could Not Come Into the House, 9 [C34]; The Bath Tub-I, 23 [C28]; The Full-Length Portrait, 28 [C32]; The Ring: A Link in a Chain, 42 [C26]; The Blond Bed, 49 [C33]; The Bath Tub-II, 61 [C28]; The Long Sunday Ride, 66; The Rain, 75 [C31]; Gentian, 87 [C39]; The Chifforobe, 104 [C35]; Ruby, Sapphire, Yellow Diamond, 121; The Glass Doors, 125; The Bath Tub-III, 136 [C28]; Myopia, 139 [C41]; The Square Jaw, 154 [A5]; Blocks and Books, 167; A Horse With Wings, 180.

Yellow and tan linenweave paper half paper boards, green half cloth spine, with author, title, and publisher lettered down spine in gold. White, blank, green, yellow and tan dust jacket with a woodcut illustration by W. Ferro of a house [duplicated on title page] in a field that extends across the jacket; subtitle not on title page: An Autobiography of Childhood; endorsements by E. M. Forster, Truman Capote, Tennessee Williams, Carl Van Vechten, James Stern, Storm Jameson, and Charles Poore on back; contents blurb on front flap continuing on back flap; biographical note and photograph by Sandy Campbell of Windham among the ruins at Delphi also on back flap.

3500 copies, of 5000 printed in December 1963, bound and published 30 January 1964. $4.50. The other 1500 were bound and issued later.

The epigraph preceding the title page, "But only to build memories of spiritual gates, "uncredited, is from Hart Crane's poem, "Emblems of Conduct." The second epigraph [ix] is from W. H. Auden's introduction to **The American Scene** by Henry James: "Above all, do not write your autobiography for your childhood is literally the whole of your capital."

b.   French limited edition

DONALD WINDHAM / Emblemes d'une vie / TRADUIT DE L'ANGLAIS PAR / elisabeth van rysselberghe / <u>nrf</u> / GALLIMARD

243 pp., 18.4 X 11.7 cm., issued with all signatures untrimmed and unopened.

[1] DU MONDE ENTIER; [2] blank; [3] title; [4, in French] 26 copies on velin pur fil Lafuma-Navarre, 1-26, English title,, rights reservation, 1968; [5] dedication; [6] blank; [7] epigraph in English; [8] blank; [9] Auden epigraph in French; [10] blank; 11-239, text; [240] blank; [241] table of contents; [242] blank; [243] Imprimerie BUSSIERE à Saint-Amand (Cher). France. -- 17-4-1968.

Pale aqua paper wrapper printed in red and black: DU MONDE ENTIER in semi-circle, DXVII in red below, title and publisher's logo; contents and price on back; glassine wrapper.

26 copies published 1968. Price unknown.

The translation suffers from several errors: "Peachtree Street" appears consistently as "Peach Street"; Windham's mother's maiden name is misspelled "Donaldsen"; "Daytona Beach" is "Drayton Beach." The back cover as well as the first page of the text indicates that Windham was "né à Alabama, Georgie."

c.   French trade edition

Identical to A8a, with the following exceptions: coated white wrapper printed in red and black; blurb on front flap with a photograph by Sandy Campbell; list of other books in the same series

on back flap; biographical note and description
on back; all edges trimmed.

Published 1968.   14fr.

A9   **TWO PEOPLE**   **1965**

a.   First edition

TWO PEOPLE / [decorative line] / A NOVEL BY /
<u>Donald Windham</u> / COWARD-McCANN, INC., NEW YORK

254 pp., 20.4 X 14.1 cm., fore-edges untrimmed.

[1] half-title; [2] list of author's publications by genre; [3] title; [4] copyright 1965
and rights reservations; [5] dedication: To
Fritz and Jeanne Bultman; [6] blank; [7] half-
title; [8] blank; 9-252, text; blank leaf.

Wine cloth boards printed in gold: author's
boxed holograph signature on front; title,
decoration, author, and publisher on spine;
bright blue endpapers. Blue, rust, and black on
white dust jacket, with an illustration of
Trinita dei Monti and the Spanish Steps in Rome
by George Salter on front and spine; endorsements by E. M. Forster, Truman Capote, Luigi
Barzini, and Tennessee Williams on back; plot
summary on front flap; photograph by Sandy
Campbell of Windham by the colonnade of Saint
Peter's Basilica in Rome, and biographical squib
on back flap.

7300 copies (of 7500 printed) published 6 August
1965, $4.95.

> Promotional copies were issued in orange
> stiff paper wrappers reprinting dust
> jacket endorsements, front and back,
> indicating "coming in August." A second
> printing of 1958 copies was issued 21
> December 1965.

b.   First English edition

TWO PEOPLE / <u>by</u> / <u>Donald Windham</u> / [publisher's
logo] / <u>London</u> / MICHAEL JOSEPH

198 pp., 19.7 X 13.6 cm. all edges trimmed.

[1] plot blurb; [2] list of author's books; [3]
title; [4] First published in Great Britain
1966; copyright 1965 by Donald Windham; [5]
dedication; [6] blank; 7-[198] text.

Teal blue pebbled paper boards with author,
decoration, title, and publisher printed in gold
on spine. Full color dust jacket illustration
by Broom Lynne of an Italian boy by the Fountain
of the Rivers, Piazza Navona in Rome, white
lettering; blurbs for other books on back;
issued with a blue band quoting E. M. Forster.

Published 10 February 1966.   25/-.

c.   Italian edition

Donald Windham / DUE VITE [in green] / Romanzo /
Traduzione di Marina Valente / ARNOLDO MONDADORI
EDITORE

224 pp., 18.8 X 10.8 cm., all edges trimmed.

[1] MEDUSA, volume 517; [2] blank; [3] title;
[4] copyright by Donald Windham, 1965, AM 1967,
Two People.; [5] half-title; [6] dedication;
[7]-218. text; [219-20] blank; [221-24] catalog
of Medusa editions.

Bright green cloth boards printed in gold: I
GRANDI NARRATORI D'OGNI PAESE [the foregoing
boxed], author, title [in a larger box], publisher [boxed, then all three enclosed in a
box]; up spine: A.M., title and author, volume
number, all separated by lines; on back, Medusa
and number 6310 in blindstamp. Green, gold,
black, and white dust jacket with Medusa head as
publisher's logo; black and white band around
the book: "uno straniero che ci vede come
siamo," Mario Soldati.

Published March 1967.   2000 lire.

d.   English paperback edition

Two People / Donald Windham / Penguin Books
176 pp., 11.2 X 18.0 cm., all edges trimmed.

[1] biographical note; [2] blank; [3] title; [4]
First published 1965, rights reservations,
Published in Penguin Books 1971; [5] dedication;
[6] blank; 7-[172] text; [173] advertisement for
Penguin Books; [174] blank; [175-76] advertise-
ments for other Penguin Books.

Stiff paper wrappers with illustration by
Michael Lackersteen of two white profiles nose
to nose, Trinita dei Monti and the Spanish Steps
in color between them; orange spine; blurbs by
E. M. Forster and Tennessee Williams on back.

Published 1971. 6/.

e.   American paperback edition

TWO PEOPLE / A NOVEL BY / Donald Windham /
POPULAR LIBRARY . NEW YORK .

256 pp., 16.4 X 10.8 cm., all edges trimmed and
stained yellow.

[1] passage from the novel, entitled "conversation piece"; [2] announcement of forthcoming
publication of **Tanaquil** and publisher's
advertisement; [3] title; [4] copyright 1965;
[5] dedication; [6] blank; [7] half-title; [8]
blank; 9-253 text; [254-56] publisher's
advertisements.

Full color stiff paper wrappers, title in blue,
with an illustration of the figure of a boy and
the head of a man against a narrow landscape of
the Spanish Steps and the Colosseum, publisher's
blurb, and quotation from **Best Sellers**, publisher's number 0-455-044292-3 and price, all on
front; plot summary and quotation from **Library
Journal** on back in black divided by FORREST /
MARCELLO / TWO PEOPLE in blue.

48,900 copies published September 1978. $1.95.

A   10   TANAQUIL   1972

a.   First edition

TANAQUIL / or / The Hardest Thing of All / <u>by</u> /

DONALD WINDHAM / <u>But if Divin Amore has wounded</u>
<u>you, then there</u> / <u>must be another beside</u>
<u>yourself; and, for that other,</u> / <u>you will gladly</u>
<u>strive, gladly suffer, gladly die, or very</u> /
<u>gladly live, which is the hardest thing of all</u>.
/ BARON CORVO / VERONA . MCMLXXII.

vi+308 pp.   23.4 X 15.3 cm., all edges trimmed.

[i-ii] blank; [iii] half-title; [iv] blank; [v]
title; [vi] copyright 1972 by Donald Windham;
[vii] dedication: To the chance encounter of
October 31st, 1942; [viii] blank; [1] Part I /
THE LEMON SQUEEZER;   3-121, text; [122] blank;
[123] Part II / GRAYWACKE; [124] blank; 125-229,
text; [230] blank; [231] Part III / PUZZLE OF
THE REWARD; [232] blank; 233-305, text; [306]
blank; [307] This first edition of <u>Tanaquil</u> has
been printed / under the supervision of Martino
Mardensteig for Sandy / Campbell by the
Stamperia Valdonega, Verona, in July / 1972.
The cover is an original lithograph by Tony
Smith, / which has been pulled from stone at the
Shorewood / Atelier, New York City, and numbered
and signed in / pencil by the artist. The
edition consists of two hundred / and fifty
copies on Favini paper; each one signed / by the
author. / This is number

Black and white lithograph print as a paper
wrapper, folded around stiff paper wrappers,
each one signed and numbered in pencil, 1/ 250,
"Tony Smith 72"; title on front, author's name
down spine; thin plastic wrapper. Sheet laid in
with endorsements of Windham's work by E. M.
Forster, Albert Camus, Thornton Wilder, Osbert
Sitwell, Georges Simenon, Paul Bowles, and Mario
Soldati. Issued in yellow coated linen slipcase.

250 copies published 31 October 1972. $75.

b.   First trade edition

TANAQUIL / A Novel by / Donald Windham / Holt,
Rinehart and Winston / New York [the foregoing
in decorative art nouveau brackets of stylized
flowers].

vi+306 pp., 20.9 X 13.5 cm., all edges trimmed.

[i] half-title; [ii] list of author's previous
books; [iii] title; [iv] Copyright 1972, 1977 by
Donald Windham, rights reservations, ISBN 0-03-
022566-3; [v] epigraph, decoration, and dedication; [vi] blank; [1] section-title [duplicating
brackets from title page]; [2] blank; 3-306,
text [including section titles with brackets pp.
123 and 231].

Dark grey paper boards with flower design from
title page embossed; white halfcloth spine with
author, title, and publisher printed down spine
in silver. Photographic dust jacket of two sil-
houetted people kissing beneath the Graywacke
Arch in Central Park, title and author in light
orange on pale orange background; author, title,
and publisher down black spine; black back with
endorsements of Windham's work by Marianne
Moore, Georges Simenon, Albert Camus, and E. M.
Forster in orange; plot summary on flaps;
author's photograph by Sandy Campbell of Windham
against the ruins at Selinute in Sicily, and
biographical sketch on back flap.

Published October 1977, $8.95.

> This edition was printed by off-set from
> Sandy Campbell's edition, but with circa
> half a dozen minor emendations and
> changes.

c.   Paperback edition

TANAQUIL / a novel by / Donald Windham / POPULAR
LIBRARY . NEW YORK

256 pp., 17.4 X 10.6 cm., all edges trimmed and
stained yellow.

[1] publisher's description, titled "PATRICIA
WAS EVEN YOUNGER THAN FRANKIE -- AND SO MUCH
OLDER"; [2] "ALSO BY DONALD WINDHAM AND
AVAILABLE FROM POPULAR LIBRARY: TWO PEOPLE
04292-3 ($1.95); [3] title; [4] Copyright 1972,
1977 by Donald Windham and rights reservation;
[5] epigraph and dedication; [6] blank; 7-256,
text. Stiff paper wrapper with full-color

illustration of a man and woman with Washington
Square arch in the background, title in blue,
and quotation from **Chicago Tribune Book World** on
front; publisher, title, author, number and
price down spine; publisher's plot summary and
review quotations on back, title in blue,
publisher's slogan in purple.

52,989 copies published October 1978. $1.95.

A 11   L'ALBERO DEI PALLONI   1974

L'ALBERO DEI PALLONI / Testo e illustrazioni di
Donald Windham / Emme Edizione.

32 pp., unpaged.   21.7 X 21.7 cm., all edges
trimmed.

[1-2], blank pastedown endpaper; [3] blank
endpaper; [4] Emme Edizioni Milano Industria
Grafiche Editoriali S.p.A. Tutti i diritti
riservati. Stampato a Venezia dalla Fan-
tonigrafica; [5] title; [6-32] text and
illustrations, printed in yellow, red, pink,
purple, green, turquoise, brown, and black.

White coated paper, boards printed with one of
the illustrations front and back; author's name,
title, and Emme Edizioni in black on front,
title and Emme Edizioni in black on spine.

Published 1974.   1500 lire.

> This children's story about a tree in
> Central Park in New York that didn't
> know its name was never published in an
> English language edition, although the
> Rizzoli Bookshop in New York imported a
> few copies of the Italian edition.
> Windham incorporated the text, in a dia-
> logue between Frankie and his son Sandy,
> in **Tanaquil** [p. 276 in A10a and A10b,
> and pp. 231-32 in A10c]. Windham exe-
> cuted the illustrations in folded and
> cut origami papers. In April 1979,
> he signed a contract for the illustra-
> tions to be used in an Italian reader
> for elementary school; nothing seems to

have come of this.

A 12   STONE IN THE HOURGLASS   1981

a.   First edition

Stone in the Hourglass [in brown] / by / DONALD
WINDHAM / VERONA MCMLXXXI

156 pp., 23.0 by 15.5 cm., all edges trimmed.

[i-ii] blank; [iii] half-title; [iv] blank; [v]
title; [vi] Copyright 1981 by Donald Windham /
ISBN 0-917366-05-0 / PRINTED ITALY; [vii]
dedication: To the future -- when time, / in
return for all it takes away, / will give us
back our lost friendships, / which will then
exist as much / as everything else that has
vanished. / And in memory of / TONY SMITH /
whose friendship I never lost.; [viii] blank;
[1] half-title; [2] blank; 3-153, text; [154]
Disclaimer Note about characters and events, and
acknowledgment to Anne Ryan for the title; [155]
blank; [156] This first edition of Stone in the
Hourglass consists / of seven hundred copies on
Ventura paper and fifty special / copies,
numbered 1-50, on Magnani paper, and was printed
/ for Sandy Campbell by the Stamperia Valdonega
in Verona / under the supervision of Martino
Mardersteig. The cover / is from a collage of
painted papers by Fritz Bultman / made
especially for this book. / MAY MCMLXXXI /
[printer's logo in brown] / This is copy number

Stiff ivory wrappers printed in red, two shades
of blue, and two shades of brown; Fritz Bultman's collage extends, in seeming mirror dupli-
cation, front and back, but the brown grounds in
the design are reversed, and the order of author
and title are reversed; title and author in
white printed up spine; thick glassine wrapper;
no endpapers.

750 copies published 2 July 1981. $15.

b.   Limited edition

Identical to A12a with the following exceptions:

50 numbered copies printed on heavy white
deckle-edged Magnani paper, 23.4 X 16 cm.,
therefore .3 cm. thicker than the first edition;
tan cloth slipcase. Published simultaneously
with the first edition. $60.

A 13   FOOTNOTE TO A FRIENDSHIP   1983

a.   First edition

FOOTNOTE / TO A FRIENDSHIP [the foregoing in
blue] / A memoir / of Truman Capote / and others
/ by / Donald Windham / VERONA MCMXXXIII

164 pp., 23.5 X 16.0 cm., all edges trimmed.

[1] blank; [2] facsimile in color [stamp
duplicating blue on title page] of a postcard
from Capote to Windham, 2 August 1978; [3]
title; [4] permission to reprint letters and
photograph, Copyright 1983 by Donald Windham /
ISBN 0-917366-06-9 / PRINTED IN ITALY; [5] list
of illustrations; [6] blank; [7] half-title and
epigraph: "Some people might have made a book /
out of it; but the story I am going to tell / is
one which it took all my strength to / live and
over which I spent all my virtue." / André Gide,
"Strait Is The Gate"; [8] blank; [9] ONE / "Be
bold. Be bold. Be not too bold" / Isak Dinesen,
"On Mottoes of My Life"; [10] blank; 11-94, text
of part one; [95] TWO / "Truth is no Apollo
Belvedere . . ." / Marianne Moore, "In the Days
of Prismatic Colour"; [96] blank; 97-137, text
of part two; [138] blank; [139] THREE / "The
armour of falsehood is / subtly wrought out of
darkness, / and hides a man not only from /
others, but from his own soul." / E. M.
Forster, "A Room with a View"; [140] blank; 141-
[161] text of part three; photographs reckoned
in pagination, 17, 21, 26, 61, 65, 77, 109, 152;
[162] blank; [163] THIS IS THE FIRST NUMBERED
EDITION OF / FOOTNOTE TO A FRIENDSHIP / IT WAS
PRINTED IN FOUR HUNDRED COPIES OF WHICH / THE
FIRST FORTY ARE ON SPECIAL BLUE FEDRIGONI PAPER
AND / ARE SIGNED BY THE AUTHOR, ALL OTHERS ARE
ON VALSUGANA / PAPER. COMPOSITION, NEGATIVES
AND PRINTING HAVE BEEN / ACCOMPLISHED IN VERONA
AT THE STAMPERIA VALDONEGA / UNDER THE

SUPERVISION OF MARTINO MARDERSTEIG / FOR SANDY
CAMPBELL / April 1983 / [printer's logo] / <u>This
is copy number</u>; [164-66] blank.

Stiff cream paper wrappers slightly larger than
text, title in blue, butterfly collage by John
Digby in black and blue, author in black on
front; title and author down spine; sub-title on
back; no endpapers.

360 copies published 13 June 1983. $35.

b.   Limited edition

Identical to A13a with the following exceptions:
Fedrigoni blue paper on which illustrations were
tipped-in. Issued in a tan stiff tan slipcase.

40 copies published 13 June 1983. $95.

> Ten additional copies were run, unnum-
> bered: three on Fedrigoni and seven on
> Valsugana, four of which -- one Fedri-
> gioni and three Valsugana -- were bound
> in a trial cover of the same design
> differently placed.

A 14   AS IF . . .   **1985**

a.   First edition

As if... [printed in brown] / <u>A personal view of</u>
/ <u>Tennessee Williams</u> / <u>by</u> / Donald Windham /
VERONA MCMLXXXV

120 pp., 23.4 X 15.9 cm., all edges trimmed.

[1] blank; [2] frontispiece; [3] title; [4]
Copyright 1985 by Donald Windham / ISBN 0-
917366-07-7 / PRINTED IN ITALY; [5] list of
illustrations; [6] blank; [7] half-title and
epigraph: "though not with bag and baggage, /
yet with scrip and scrippage," / <u>William
Shakespeare</u>, / "<u>As You Like It</u>"; [8] blank; [9]
ONE / "For the dead, who seem to take away / so
much, really take with them noth-/ ing that is
ours. The passion they have / aroused lives
after them, easy to transmute / or to transfer,

but well-nigh impossible / to destroy." / <u>E. M.
Forster</u>, / "<u>Where Angels Fear to Tread</u>"; [10]
blank; 11-61, text of part one; [62] blank; [63]
TWO / "Migrations that must void the memory, /
Inventions that cobblestone the heart . . ." /
<u>Hart Crane,</u> / "<u>The Bridge</u>" / I. Text of the
first edition, The Black Sun PRess, Paris 1930.;
[64] blank; 65-88, text of part two; [89] THREE
/ "Society knows very well how to go / about
suppressing a man and has meth- / ods more
subtle than death." / <u>André Gide,</u> / "<u>In
Memoriam: Oscar Wilde</u>"; [89] blank; [90]
illustration; 91-[117] text of part three; other
illustrations reckoned in pagination [19, 37,
55, 73, 91]; [118] blank; [119] THIS FIRST
EDITION OF / "AS IF..." / CONSISTS OF THREE
HUNDRED COPIES, OF WHICH FIFTY / SPECIAL COPIES,
NUMBERED 1-50, ARE ON FAVA PAPER, / SIGNED BY
THE AUTHOR, AND TWO HUNDRED / FIFTY COPIES,
NUMBERED 51-300, ARE ON BODONIA PAPER. / IT WAS
PRINTED BY THE STAMPERIA VALDONEGA IN / VERONA
UNDER THE SUPERVISION OF MARTINO / MARDERSTEIG
FOR SANDY CAMPBELL / June 1985 / [printer's
logo] / <u>This is copy number</u>; [120] blank.

Stiff brown paper wrappers, title in grey,
butterfly collage by John Digby in grey and
black, author's name in black on front; title
and author in white on spine; sub-title in white
on back; no endpapers.

250 copies published 1 August 1985. $35.

b.   Limited edition

Identical to A14a with the following exceptions:
Fava paper, on which the illustrations were
tipped-in; fore-edges uneven; 23.7 X 16.4 cm.

Issued in tan fava paper slipcase.

50 copies published 1 August 1985. $95.

A 15   LOST FRIENDSHIPS   1987

a.   First edition

[line] / [the following, including the dots,

boxed in a line] L͟ . O͟ . S͟ . T͟ / FRIENDSHIPS
/ [line] / A Memoir of Truman Capote, /
Tennessee Williams, and Others / [dot] / DONALD
WINDHAM / William Morrow and Company, Inc. New
York

272 pp., 23.4 X 15.5 cm., all edges trimmed.

[1] half-title; [2] blank; [3] list of the
author's previous publications; [4] blank; [5]
title; [6] Copyright 1983, 1985, 1987 by Donald
Windham / "Most of the material appearing in
this book has been printed privately by Sandy
Campbell in Italy in two volumes: Footnote to a
Friendship and As if . . . : A Personal View of
Tennessee Williams," rights reservations, ISBN
0-688-06947-9, first edition [7] table of
contents; [8] blank; 9-10, illustrations; 11-12,
Foreword; [13] epigraph: ". . . youth, strength,
genius, thoughts, achievements, simple hearts --
all die . . . no matter." Joseph Conrad,
"Youth"; [14] blank; [15] half-title, the
subtitle deleting Tennessee Williams's name;
[16] blank; [17] facsimile of postcard from
Truman Capote to Donald Windham, 2 August 1978;
[18] permission to reprint letters; [19] Gide
epigraph; [20] blank; [21] ONE, Dinesen epigraph
[here and in subsequent epigraphs, roman and
italic type in A13 and A14 printed in reverse];
[22] blank; 23-267, text; 268-70, Afterword;
[271] blank; [271-72] blank; photographs printed
on coated stock signatures, gathered and
reckoned in pagination [97-104] and [201-08].

Grey paper boards, blue quarter-cloth spine,
with author, title and publisher letters on
spine in silver; blue endpapers. Blue dust
jacket printed in peach and silver on front;
white back with endorsements by Harper Lee, Paul
Bowles, Robert Lewis, and James Merrill. Content summary on front flap; photograph by Joan
Digby of Windham on Fire Island, and biographical squib on back flap.

Published 25 February 1987, $17.95.

        Unaccountably, the publisher altered E.
        E. Cummings to e. e. Cummings and cor-
        rupted some Italian spellings and place-

names. Windham made several corrections
and revisions for **Lost Friendships**.
Pages and lines follow changes. From
Footnote to a Friendship: "was begun six
years ago" (11.10) to "was begun in
1977" (23.10); "to make him" (19.15)) to
"to label him" (23.26); "cowered" (24.1)
to "cowed" (32.38); "Mitsouka" (24.9-10)
to "Mitsouko" (33.1-2); "Sunday New York
Times" (46.16) to "N.Y. Times Book
Review" (51.15-16); "not a masochist it
was wise" (51.19-20) to "not a masochist
or an opportunist it was wise" (56.7);
"he did not think my attitude such that
he would ask my advice about something
he was working on" (52.18-19) to "it was
not until this year with 'A Christmas
Memory,' a story as real as Chekhov's.
that he won my unreserved admiration"
(56-57); "Sandy to them in a" (76.19) to
"Sandy to them separately in a" (76.16-
17); "his right eye" (86.2) to "his left
eye" (84.4); "instinctly" (103.18) to
"instinctively" (108.18); "letters, I
would" (106.3) to "letters, which I
doubted, I would" (110.26-27); "including a telegram" (129.18) to "following a
telegram: (131.18); "a 'funny story'"
(142.5) to "an equally fictitious 'funny
story'" (142.7-8). From **As if . . . :**
"laughter lost" (11.17) to "early laughter lost" (167.16-17); "four years
later" (22.15) to "five years later"
(176.17); "returned in the fall" (28.3)
to "returned in November" (181.3); "is
fall again" (28.25) to "is midwinter"
(181.24); "He is leaving for New
Orleans" (29.12-13) to "He is leaving"
(182.13; "The next spring" (29.14) to
"Early next spring" (182.14); "This time
Tennessee has arrived without sufficient
funds to rent a room" (29.18-19) to
"Tennessee by this time is without sufficient funds to rent a room even if he
wants to" (182.18-19); "drunken night"
(30.19) to "fagging night" (183.13); "on
its roof" (32.20) to "overlooking its
roof" (185.2-3); "This subject recurs
later. It is worth saying here that

whatever preponderance of the work on
the play was his" (38. footnote) to "It
is worth saying here . . . was Tennessee's" (190. footnote); "It is a
Saturday" (40.9) to "It is Easter eve"
(192.5); "Laura has less kinship" to
"For example, Laura has less kinship,"
and "is nearer to the narrator's" to "is
nearer to the brother's" (41. footnote,
193. footnote); "of recognition and
suspicion" (42.27-28) to "of recognition
and self-protection" (194.13-14);
"Divorced from his wife" (45.16) to
"Divorced from his wife in Georgia"
(197.19-20); "His affair with Kip"
(56.4) to "I think his affair with Kip"
(222.6).

b.   Second printing

Identical to A15a excepting deletion [6] of
first edition line.

c.   Paperback edition

Identical to A15a, with the following exceptions: [5] [publisher's logo] / PARAGON HOUSE /
NEW YORK; [6] First paperback edition, 1989,
publisher's address, ISBN 1-55778-240-7; pagination identical but photographs printed on text
stock. 22.7 X 15.0 cm. Stiff paper wrappers
printed in black, brown, and white on pale
melon, with three of the photographs color-
tinted on front, designed by Irving Freeman;
endorsements by Kirkus Service, Harper Lee, Paul
Bowles, and James Merrill, with a content summary and biographical squib on back.

Published 1989, $10.95.

The publisher corrected Morrow's gaffe
over E. E. Cummings and several but not
all others.

A 16   THE ROMAN SPRING OF ALICE TOKLAS   1987

THE ROMAN SPRING / OF / ALICE TOKLAS [the

foregoing in wine] / <u>44 Letters by Alice Toklas</u> / <u>in a Remembrance by</u> / <u>Donald Windham</u> / VERONA MCMLXXXVII

75 pp., 23.8 X 15.8 cm., all edges trimmed.

[1-3] blank; [4] facsimile of a holograph letter from Alice Toklas to Sandy Campbell, 24 May 1951; [5] title; [6] Front and back covers are reproduced from / botanical drawings attributed to Pieter Holsteyne / the Younger (1614-1687): "Viola" and "Dobbelde / violet, groote witte violet, violet admirant". / Letters of Alice B. Toklas Copyright 1987 / by Edward Burns / Reminiscence Copyright 1987 / by Donald Windham / ISBN 0-917366-08-5 / Printed in Italy; [7] list of illustrations; [8] blank; [9] half-title; [10] blank; 11-72, text; illustrations reckoned in pagination [17, 20-21, 23, 29, 31, 40, 42, 44, 68]; [73] blank; [174] This first edition of / THE ROMAN SPRING OF ALICE TOKLAS / consists of two hundred copies numbered 1-200 / printed on Bodonia paper under the supervision / of Martino Mardersteig by the Stamperia / Valdonega, Verona, for / Sandy Campbell. / October 1987 / [printer's logo] / <u>This is copy number</u>; [74-75] blank.

Stiff ivory paper wrapper: front centers a full color drawing of violets between duplicated title, and subtitle and author, from title page; a full color drawing of three anemones on back; title and author down spine. Acetate wrapper; no endpapers. Issued in a brown stiff paper slipcase.

200 copies published 31 October 1987. $35.

Five unnumbered copies were run.

Your new writing is better
old arrangement is better

works unless they are hugh crazy negros like George. *[the white men make him self-conscious]*

    "You'll be having a big week end," answered *[the negro]* George. He wiped the sweat from around his eyes and laughed, *[His]* swinging ~~his~~ body ~~and~~ glistening all over.

    "Might get a pint to take home. Got to save some. The way Scarrett hates to see a renny of the company's money go as bad as if it were his own, I bet he's as mad as hell."

    "Yes sir, Mis'er Williams." George was still smiling and he said carefully, "If you going to put some of h *shed* that away, I ~~sure~~ could use a little till next week. I ain't lying, Mis'er Williams, and I'll tell you the truth of what I want it for. I's buying me a second hand automobile to ride to work in, and take my wife out riding on Sundays, and if you lets me borrow three dollars to make the payment this week I'll give it back to you next Friday."

    "Yeah," said Williams, " how the hell ~~are~~ you going to have more money next week than this?" *[when disgusted] [why here?]*

    "I just got to pay my doctor bill ~~this week~~, Mister Williams, Last month when I was sick at work with the piles Mis'er Scarrett took me to his doctor instead of the company's. I didn't know nothing about it and now I got to pay him this week or he's going to sue me."

    Williams leaned over the iron backbar of George's machine. "Why don't you borrow it from Scarrett. He's got pleanty of money. I haven't."

    [just won of a lit] "He wont lend it to me. I asked him, ~~and~~ told him

"The Warm Country," 1940, manuscript page with holograph suggestions by Tennessee Williams

The Warm Country, 1960, dust jacket design for the first edition [A7a] by Heather Standring

EMBLEMS OF CONDUCT

by Donald Windham

CHARLES SCRIBNER'S SONS, *New York*

Emblems of Conduct, 1963, title page design for the first edition [A8a] by W. Ferro

Tanaquil, 1972, original lithograph wrapper for the first edition [A10a] by Tony Smith, numbered and signed by the artist

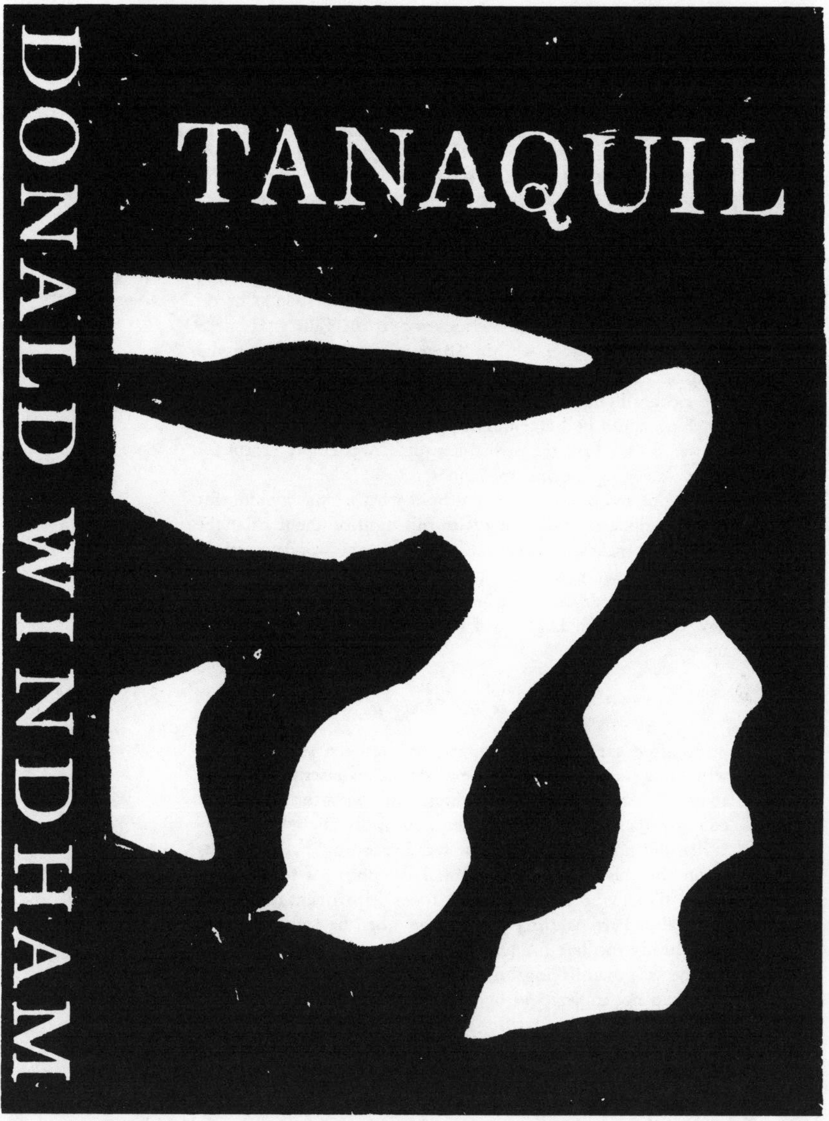
TANAQUIL
DONALD WINDHAM

He had waited at a telephone booth on a
nearby corner - the same corner the ambulance
carrying Julia Farr from the Medical Center to
the nursing home will pass on its way to Seward
Park a week later - until he received Dietrich's
call that Parsons was at the gallery. Then he
had, with effort, hurried to the apartment. He need,

new copy above

degree that pleased his lazy liking for privilege and adventure.
~~He had with efforts, hurried to the apartment from the nearby~~
~~telephone booth where he had been waiting, as soon as he re-~~
~~ceived Dietrich's call that Parsons was at the gallery. He need~~
not have been in such a rush. There was only one room and a
bath, and the room contained not a single chest or closet. The
few clothes hung from hooks on the wall. There was no place
anything could be hidden. The bricks-and-planks desk had no
drawer. In the bath the medicine cabinet was empty except for
razors, shaving lotions, medicines.

follow proof

The one receptacle that could hold what he was looking for
was a cardboard box of papers in full sight on the floor at the
side of the makeshift desk. He pulled out the wooden straight
chair, sat down, and leaned over the box to see if it contained
what he wanted. On the top sheet the title of Digby Jones's
new novel, which Digby had been talking to him about, met
his eye.

Stone in the Hourglass

He lifted the sheet and looked through the stack of type-
written pages beneath. They were not the manuscript of a book
about Walter Farr and his daughter. They were the manuscript
of a novel, and the novel was unquestionably Digby's.

Red did not understand what was happening, but he under-
stood that his luck was holding. His upturn of fortune had
begun the day he went to Digby Jones's apartment to pick up
the Walter Farr painting - at a time when he had thought it
was already too late for him to be lucky, and when he feared
that he was overplaying his hand.

He did not understand by what coincidence the man whom
Dietrich thought was writing a book about Walter Farr was a
man who had stolen the manuscript of Digby's novel. But

152

Stone in the Hourglass, 1981, page proof with corrections by Donald Windham

B. Books and Pamphlets with Contributions

B 1   NEW DIRECTIONS 10   **1948**
           IN PROSE AND POETRY

a.   First edition

New / Directions / 10 / in prose and poetry [the foregoing in cursive facsimile holograph] / AN ANNUAL EXHIBITION GALLERY OF NEW / AND DIVERGENT TRENDS IN LITERATURE / New Directions

512 pp., 22.8 X 15.1 cm., all edges trimmed.

[1] half-title; [2] editor's note; [3] title; [4] copyright and acknowledgments; [5] dedication to Alfred and Blanche Knopf; [6-7] contents; [8] blank; 9-16, Notes on Contributors; 17-22, 510-12, A Few Random Notes from the Editor; 23-509, text.

Buff linen boards stamped in wine on spine: N / D / 1 0; coated white dust jacket printed in black.

Published 1948. $4.50.

CONTAINS: "Flesh Farewell," pp. 94-102. [A7]

b.   Reprint edition

Identical to B1a, with the following exceptions: [3] KRAUS REPRINT CORPORATION / New York / 1967;

[4] permission acknowledgment to New Directions
Publishing Corporation; black cloth binding,
title in gold on green block; date, number, and
decorative bands in gold. 22.3 X 14.3 cm.

Published 1967. $46.

B 2   KAREN BLIXEN   **1962**

a.   First (Danish) edition

KAREN BLIXEN / Redigeret af / Clara Svendsen og
Ole Wivel / Gyldendal / 1962

229 pp., 24.2 X 16.5 cm., all edges trimmed.

[1] half-title; [2] full-page frontispiece
photograph of Karen Blixen by Jesper Hom, 1961,
tipped-in; [3] title; [4] copyright 1962; 5-[6]
table of contents; 7-229, text.

Stiff gray paper wrappers, title and publisher
from title page in black; clear wrapper attached
over marbled green and silver dust jacket with
full photograph of Karen Blixen by Cecil Beaton,
1962, on front.

Published 1962.   kr. 32,000 1.0.

CONTAINS: "Tre aftener i Rom," pp. 143-44.

b.   American edition

ISAK DINESEN / [decoration] / A MEMORIAL /
Edited by Clara Svendsen / [publisher's logo] /
RANDOM HOUSE NEW YORK

214 pp., 20.8 X 13.2 cm., all edges trimmed.

Blank leaf; unreckoned leaf, half-title on
recto, blank verso; [i] blank; [ii] small
photograph of Karen Blixen as a frontispiece;
[iii] title; [iv] copyrights, reservations,
first printing; v-vii, table of contents; [viii]
blank; [1] half-title; [2] blank; 3-209, text;
[210] blank; two blank leaves.

Black cloth boards; blind decorations on front;

printed in gold down spine with decorations,
title, editor, publisher's logo, and name;
orange top edges; green endpapers. Cream dust
jacket, title and editor printed in black and
stylized flowers printed in red on front; titles
and prices of seven of Isak Dinesen's books
listed on back; assessment of the writer and her
work on front and back flaps.

Published 1965. $4.50.

CONTAINS: "Three Nights in Rome," pp. 81-82.

> The Danish edition contains twenty-seven
> contributions by Danes omitted from the
> American edition.   Further, all contri-
> butions are in Danish.   In the American
> edition most of them are printed in the
> languages in which they were written.

B 3   PUBLISHER'S CHOICE   1967

PUBLISHER'S / CHOICE [seven sunbursts] / Ten
Short Story Discoveries By / The Editors of
Scribners / Charles Scribner's Sons / New York

251 pp., 20.9 X 13.9 cm., all edges trimmed.

[1] half-title; [2] blank; [3] title; [4]
copyright and credits; 5-[6] table of contents;
7-10, introductory biographies; [11] half-title;
[12] blank; 13-251, text.

Turquoise (one third) and black (two thirds)
cloth boards printed on front and down spine in
silver; one silver and two red sunbursts at
title; turquoise, red, black, and white dust
jacket with authors listed on back.

Published 1967. $4.95

CONTAINS: "The Starless Air," pp. 173-203.
             [A7]

> The copyright page lists "The Starless
> Air," as "Copyright 1960 by Noonday
> Press," but the only story ever
> published by Noonday Press was "The

Third Bridge" in the periodical **Noonday**.
This may be a deliberate error; see A7.

B 4   AMERICA, THE MELTING POT   1969

America, the Melting Pot / <u>Edited by</u> / PATRICIA
POMBOY MINTZ / ILLUSTRATIONS BY / JAMES AND RUTH
MCCREA / CHARLES SCRIBNER'S SONS. NEW YORK

318 pp., 20.2 X 14.2 cm., all edges trimmed.

[i] half-title; [ii] The American Character
Series; [iii] title; [iv] copyrights and
acknowledgments; [v] acknowledgments; [vi]
blank; [vii] dedication: for Peter; [viii]
blank; 1-318, text. In some copies on the last
page, in some copies on the inside back cover:
Scribner Student Paperbacks [followed by a list
of titles].

Stiff, full color coated paper wrappers, with
illustration of immigrants on front and back:
"Scribner Student Paperback."

Published 1969. $2.40.

CONTAINS: "Paolo," pp. 221-34 [A7, C27, C37]
            preceded by critical and biographical
            notes, and followed by questions
            about the text for teaching.

B 5   E. M. FORSTER'S LETTERS   1975
**   TO DONALD WINDHAM**

E. M. FORSTER'S / LETTERS TO / DONALD WINDHAM
[the foregoing in orange] / <u>With comments</u> / <u>by</u>
<u>the recipient</u> / VERONA MCMLXXV

48 pp., 23.5 X 16.0 cm., fore-edges and lower
edges untrimmed.

[1-2] blank; [3] title; [4] ALL RIGHTS RESERVED
/ THE LETTERS OF THE LATE E. M. FORSTER ARE
PRINTED / WITH PERMISSION OF THE TRUSTEES OF HIS
ESTATE. / COPYRIGHT 1975 THE PROVOST AND
SCHOLARS / OF KING'S COLLEGE CAMBRIDGE / PRINTED

IN ITALY; 5, introductory note; [6] holograph facsimile of a note dated June 1948; 7-36, text; [37] photograph of Forster and Windham at Cambridge by Sandy Campbell; 1960; 38-[46] text; [47] blank; [48] THREE HUNDRED COPIES OF / E. M. FORSTER'S LETTERS TO DONALD WINDHAM / HAVE BEEN PRINTED FOR SANDY CAMPBELL / UNDER THE SUPERVISION OF MARTINO MARDERSTEIG / BY THE STAMPERIA VALDONEGA / VERONA . OCTOBER 1975 / [printer's logo]; blank leaf.

Stiff buff paper wrapper; title duplicated in orange on front above "All good wishes. / Yours sincerely / E M Forster" in holograph facsimile; title down spine; "Love from / Morgan" in holograph facsimile on back.

300 copies published October 1975. $17.50.

CONTAINS: a running commentary before and
          between the letters.

B 6   **TENNESSEE WILLIAMS' LETTERS**   1976
         TO DONALD WINDHAM, 1940-65

a.   First edition

TENNESSEE WILLIAMS' / LETTERS TO / DONALD WINDHAM / 1940-65 [the foregoing in blue] / Edited and with comments / by / DONALD WINDHAM / VERONA MCLXXVI [sic, MCMLXXVI]

xiv+334 pp., 24.3 X 16.7 cm., all edges trimmed.

[blank leaf, on verso] facsimile of a holograph envelope from Williams to Windham, printed in color; [i] title; [ii] ALL RIGHTS RESERVED / THE LETTER TO KENNETH TYNAN COPYRIGHT 1976 / BY TENNESSEE WILLIAMS / ALL OTHER LETTERS AND COMMENTS COPYRIGHT 1976 / BY DONALD WINDHAM / ISBN 0-917366-01-8 / PRINTED IN ITALY; [iii] epigraph: The loveliest thing that can occur to me in the Bicentennial year is our resumed contact -- I needed it so badly -- and the letters to bind it all back together. Love, Tennessee, January 9, 1976; [v] half-title; [vi] blank; vii-xiii, Introduction; [1] half-title; [2] blank; 3-323, text; [324] blank; 325-33,

index; [334] blank; [335] FIVE HUNDRED NUMBERED
COPIES OF / <u>TENNESSEE WILLIAMS' LETTERS TO</u> /
<u>DONALD WINDHAM</u> / ON FAVINI PAPER / AND TWENTY-
SIX COPIES LETTERED A TO Z / ON BLUE FABRIANO
PAPER / HAVE BEEN PRINTED FOR SANDY CAMPBELL /
UNDER THE SUPERVISION OF MARTINO MARDERSTEIG /
BY THE STAMPERIA VALDONEGA / VERONA . 8
SEPTEMBER 1976 / [printer's logo in blue] THIS
IS COPY NUMBER; illustrations between the
following pages: 24-25, facsimile of typed and
holograph letter in pencil, 24 February 1942;
156-57, four-page facsimile in color in holo-
graph letter in ink, 18 December 1944; 296-97,
facsimile of a drawing in blue ink, holograph
caption in red ink, "A Happy New Year! -- 10."
December 1958.

Stiff cream paper wrapper, under a second stiff
cream wrapper with a photographic cover in full
color of eight of Williams's holograph return
addresses on the front and six on the back;
title in blue on spine. Issued in blue cloth
slipcase.

526 copies published 8 September 1976. $50.

CONTAINS: "Introduction," section headnotes,
           extensive footnotes, and "Appendix."

           Eight additional copies on Favini were
           prepared, identical to the other 500,
           marked in ink "OUT OF SERIES." Two went
           to the Library of Congress for copy-
           right; three were dismantled by Holt,
           Rinehart, and Winston for use in a trade
           offset edition.

b.   Limited edition

Identical to B6a, but as described in its
colophon and signed by Tennessee Williams and
Donald Windham. $175.

c.   First trade edition

TENNESSEE / WILLIAMS' LETTERS / TO DONALD /
WINDHAM / 1940-1965 / Edited and with comments /
by / DONALD WINDHAM / Holt, Rinehart and Winston
/ New York

Pagination identical to B6a with the following
exceptions: [i] half-title; [ii] facsimile not
printed in color; [iii] title; [iv] Copyright
1976, 1977 by Donald Windham, Kenneth Tynan
letter copyright 1976 by Tennessee Williams, all
other letters and comments copyright 1976, 1977
by Donald Windham; ISBN 0-03-022636-8; v-xi,
Introduction; [xii] blank; [1] half-title and
epigraph; 3-333, text. The reproductions of the
illustrations are collected together, crudely
printed, between pp. 168-69.

xii+334 pp., 22.8 X 15.0 cm., all edges trimmed.

Pale teal paper boards with TW/DW printed in
gold in lower right hand corner; white linen
quarter cloth spine, title lettered down in two
lines, publisher lettered across, in gold;
coated white dust jacket, title in pale teal,
facsimile return address on front and seven
return addresses on back, all printed in black
on irregular tan scraps to suggest torn
envelopes; content blurb on flaps; photograph by
Sandy Campbell of Williams and Windham in Campo
dei Fiori, Rome, 1948, on back flap.

Published 1977. $10.00.

> Windham made a few minor alterations for
> the trade edition: "more of my life"
> (xi.4) to "more of life" (ix.4); follow-
> ing "Battle of Angels" (4.8), "and thus
> adding another $100 a month to his
> income" (4.8); "received a telegram
> informing him" (4.11) to "received a
> telegram from Lawrence Langner and
> Theresa Helburn informing him" (4.11);
> "Maria Britneva, young actress and
> adventuress, friend of Tennessee's from
> this time on" (236. footnote) to "Maria
> Britneva, young actress and friend of
> Tennessee's from this time on" (236.
> footnote). Sandy Campbell's edition is
> not credited on the copyright page
> because Williams had announced his
> intention to sue both Windham and Holt,
> Rinehart, and Winston at the time. Even
> though Windham doubted Williams's
> threat, he did not wish to involve Camp-

bell in any legal action.

d.   Paperback edition

Identical to B6c, with the following exceptions:
[i] PENGUIN BOOKS (in place of prior publisher);
silver, black, and magenta stiff paper wrappers,
with three illustrations on front and blurbs and
reviews on back.   19.5 X 12.7 cm.

Published 1980. $4.95.

> Windham made a few additional changes
> for the paperback edition: Jack
> Dunphy's name, which had been cut, was
> restored (234);   cuts about Gore Vidal
> were restored: in the following
> sentence, "Since then he has divided his
> time between the [. . .] and the notices
> of his latest book: I don't know which
> excites him the more but I suspect that
> the [. . .] taste better," the word
> "sailors" replaces the ellipses (252);
> "She was an actress until she married
> the Lord St Just, then she became the
> Lady St. Just" (Williams, <u>Memoirs</u>, p.
> 149)" (236. footnote).

> The long history of the evolution of
> this book has been spelled out in much
> of the material documented in Sections
> A, C, and E of this bibliography.
> Williams granted Windham permission in
> writing -- his signature witnessed -- to
> edit and publish the letters, assigning
> the copyright to Windham for his labors,
> having been given them for a period of
> time to reread beforehand; then on
> publication he protested their appear-
> ance. The reader wishing to follow the
> route of this painful but remarkable
> literary contretemps is directed
> especially to the following entries:
> A13, A14, A15, C53, C54, C57, D12, E104,
> E109, E111, E114, E115, E119, E120,
> E121.

B 7   JOSEPH CORNELL COLLAGES 1931-1972   1978

JOSEPH / CORNELL / [line] / COLLAGES / 1931-1972
[all of the foregoing in a octagonal box] / With
texts by / Donald Windham / and / Howard Hussey
/ Introduction by / Richard L. Feigen /
CASTELLI.FEIGEN.CORCORAN [all of the foregoing
in a one-line border]

128 pp.   20.3 X 15 cm., all edges trimmed.

[1] half-title; [2] blank; [3] title; [4]
copyrights 1978 and credits; [5] contents; [6]
blank; [7] Acknowledgments; [8] photograph of
Cornell; 9-24, introductory essays; 25, catalogue and illustrations; [26] blank; 27-125,
text and illustrations; [126-28] blank
[Beginning with the title page, all pages have
single lines top and bottom -- including blank
pages; illustrations are boxed in with single
vertical lines.]

Stiff slate-brown paper wrapper engraved in
white on front and spine; gray wove fly-leaf
front and back.

3000 copies published 1978.

CONTAINS: "Things That Cannot Be Said," pp. 11-
            13.

            The text of Windham's tribute was based
            on a speech he gave at the memorial
            service for Joseph Cornell at the
            Metropolitan Museum of Art, 15 January
            1973.

B 8   THE MEANING OF LIFE   1988

The Meaning of / <u>Life</u> / Collected by Hugh S.
Moorhead / Chicago Review Press

iv+236 pp., 17.8 X 12.5 cm., all edges trimmed.

[i] title; [ii] Library of Congress Cataloging-
in-Publication Data; ISBN 1-556-52038-7; copyright information; [iii] dedication; [iv] blank;
1-6, introduction; [7] "Please comment on the
question, what is the meaning or the purpose of
life"; [8] blank; 9-227, responses; [228] blank;

229-32, acknowledgments; [233-36] blank.
White cloth boards with title, collector's name,
and publisher printed down spine in black.
Published 1988, $14.95.

CONTAINS: holograph letter from Windham to
             Moorhead reproduced in facsimile, p.
             225, dated 2/2/78; the text of the
             letter minus salutation and closing,
             plus a passage from **Tanaquil**, p.
             224.

**B 9   MRS. JOYCE OF ZURICH AND   1989
           MR. FORSTER OF KING'S**

MRS. JOYCE OF ZURICH / AND / MR. FORSTER OF
KING'S [all of the foregoing in green] / by /
SANDY CAMPBELL / VERONA MCMXXXIX

88 pp., 23.4 X 15.8 cm., all edges trimmed.

[1-4] blank; [5] half-title; [6] color photograph of leaves from Joyce's grave; [7] title;
[8] On the cover: Pen and ink drawing of Sandy
Campbell / by Paul Cadmus, 1943, / reprint
credits, copyrights 1952, 1964 by Sandy
Campbell, copyright 1989 by Donald Windham, ISBN
0-917366-09-3/ PRINTED IN ITALY; [9] table of
contents; [10] blank; [11] list of illustrations; [12] blank; 13-[17] Foreword; [18]
blank; [19] half-title: Mrs. Joyce of Zurich;
[20] blank; 21-30, text; [31] half-title: Mr.
Forster of King's; [32] blank; 33-50; [51] half-
title: The Lunts of Genesee Depot, [52] blank;
53-79, text; [80] blank; [81] This numbered
first edition of / MRS. JOYCE OF ZURICH AND MR.
FORSTER OF KING'S / consists of two hundred
fifty copies printed on / Bodonia paper for
Donald Windham under / the supervision of
Martino Mardersteig / by the Stamperia Valdonega
/ Verona. / October 1989 / [printer's logo] <u>This
is copy number</u> [number printed in]; [82] blank;
[83] catalogue of Sandy Campbell's Stamperia
Valdonega Editions; [84] blank; two blank
leaves; illustrations pp. 17,37,43,67.

Heavy cream wrapper, under a stiff cream wrapper
with title printed in green and pen and ink

drawing of Sandy Campbell and author's name in
black; title and author printed down spine in
black; acetate dust wrapper.   Issued in a green
paper slipcase.

Published October 1989. $35.

CONTAINS: "Foreword," pp. 13-17.

> "Mrs. Joyce of Zurich" originally
> appeared in **Harper's Bazaar**, October
> 1952, 170-71; "Mr. Forster of King's"
> originally appeared in **Mademoiselle**,
> June 1964, 80-81.   Donald Windham
> arranged and edited for publication "The
> Lunts of Genesee Depot" from Sandy
> Campbell's notes and first draft.

C. Contributions to Periodicals

C 1   [review] **Love, Here is My Hat**, by
       William Saroyan, **Boys' High Tatler**,
       Atlanta, Georgia, 1936.

C 2   [review] **My War With the United States**,
       by Ludwig Bemelmans, **Boys' High Tatler**,
       Atlanta, Georgia, 18 May 1938.

C 3   El Septimo Dia ["The Seventh Day" A7],
       Sur [Argentina], September 1943, 32-41.
       The magazine was banded, announcing
       Windham's story; elsewhere in the
       magazine, another was announced for a
       subsequent issue -- "El pais calido"
       ["The Warm Country" A7] -- but it was
       never published in **Sur**.

C 4   Comment, **Dance Index**, August 1943 [99].
       In this and subsequent issues of the
       periodical, Windham was responsible for
       much of the editorial work, layout,
       photographs and illustrations; from 1944
       until March 1946 he was solely
       responsible (C6, C7, C9, C10, C12).
       Some of this labor was later
       appropriated by Paul Magriel, but
       without crediting Windham, for his
       monographs on Isadora Duncan, Vaslav
       Nijinsky, and Anna Pavlova.

C 5   Night, **View**, December 1943, centerfold,

84-85. This orange leaf, printed
horizontally down both pages and titled
"Children's Page," carried selections by
other writers as well.

C 6   The Stage and Ballet Designs of Pavel
       Tchelitchew, **Dance Index**, January-
       February 1944, 4-30.

C 7   Comment, **Dance Index**, July-August 1944
       [103], unsigned.

C 8   The Eyes of Ulysses, **View**, Summer 1944,
       44. This anthology is of 209
       descriptions of eyes from James Joyce's
       Ulysses.

C 9   Comment, **Dance Index**, December 1944
       [215], unsigned.

C 10   Comment, **Dance Index**, January 1945 [3],
       unsigned.

C 11   Letter to the Editor [about various
       literary articles, notably one on James
       Joyce, in the 4 December 1944 issue],
       New Republic, 8 January 1945, 56.

C 12   Notes on Choreography, by George
       Balanchine, **Dance Index**, February-March
       1945, 20-31. These "Notes," ghost-
       written by Windham for Balanchine, went
       through several drafts, each of which
       Balanchine criticized and amplified
       orally as they progressed. He had been
       hesitant about his command of the
       English language.

C 13   A Dark Riddle, **View**, May 1946, 68. This
       collection of passages describing night
       were framed in a drawing by Corrado
       Cagli. The writers included Hart Crane,
       Shakespeare, Joyce, Thoreau, Whitman,
       Michael Drayton, and D. H. Lawrence,
       among others.

C 14   The Warm Country, **Horizon** [England] 15,
       June 1947, 313+23. [A7, C38]

C 15   El Buho y Picasso, **Americana**, September
        1947, 31.
        This is a Spanish translation of
        Windham's "The Owl and Picasso." The
        periodical, printed in the United
        States, was distributed only in Paris,
        Havana, and Buenos Aires.

C 16   Single Harvest, **Horizon** [England],
        October 1947, 84-89. [A7]

C 17   Rosebud, **Horizon** [England], July 1949,
        13-30. [A7]

C 18   The New Moon With the Old Moon in Her
        Arms, **The Listener** [England] 5, 3 May
        1951, 719-21. [A7, C20]

C 19   An Island of Fire, **Botteghe Oscure**
        [Italy] VII, 1951, 277-91 [A7]
        This multi-lingual literary journal of
        book-length issues, was published twice
        yearly in Rome, featuring -- in
        retrospect -- a distinguished list of
         contributors. This issue for example
        contained work by Elsa Morante, Truman
        Capote, and Albert Camus.

C 20   The New Moon With the Old Moon in Her
        Arms, **Mademoiselle**, January 1952, 120.
        [A7, C18] Turned down because it was
        "not up to" Windham's "usual high
        standing" by **Mademoiselle**, this story
        was then picked up after it had appeared
        in **The Listener**. That "high standing"
        had never been high enough for
        Mademoiselle to accept anything
        previously.

C 21   Rome, **Paris Review**, Autumn 1953, 95-112.
        This story is the second section of a
        three-part novella titled "Fichi
        d'India." It is about an American
        composer who has come to Italy to write
        an opera based on Nathaniel Hawthorne's
        The Marble Faun. The other sections,
        which occur in Florence and Taormina,
        have not been published. **Paris Review**
        gave the title "Rome" to this section.

C 22   Letter to the Editor [about distorting liberties taken in the dramatization by Ruth and Augustus Goetz of **The Immoralist** by Andre Gide], **New York Times**, 20 February 1954.

C 23   To Three Italians: To R . . . ; To T . . . ; To F . . . , **Folder** 1, #2, April 1954.
Printed on a folded and unnumbered leaf, these poems addressed to three Italian cities, were included with similarly separately printed works by, among others, John Ashbery, Frank O'Hara, Kenneth Koch, and Arthur Gregor. **Folder** is a periodical only because of its date. The paper and typography are superior and the individ-ual contributions are not bound together. Clearly, the production was designed with bibliophiles in mind, and there are no advertisements.

C 24   A Note on Anne Ryan, **Botteghe Oscure** [Italy] XXII, 1958, 267-71.
This reminiscence and biographical essay, written to accompany her story, "The Darkest Leaf," concentrated on Ryan's writings rather than on her graphic art.

C 25   Rome, **Cronache** [Italy], 9 November 1954, 30-31. This is an abbreviated version of C21, translated into Italian.

C 26   The Ring: A Link in a Chain, **The Listener** [England] 61, 5 March 1959, 411-12. [A8]

C 27   Paolo, **The Listener** [England] 61, 2 April 1959, 600-02. [A7, B4, C37]

C 28   The Bathtub, **The Listener** [England] 62, 16 July 1959, 101-3. [A8]

C 29   A Key to André Gide, by Pierre Herbart, translated by Windham with a note, **Noonday** 2, April 1959, 33-34.
A translation of Herbart's **À la**

recherche d'André Gide includes Windham's two-page introductory note on the recurring traits which make a person become a writer.

C 30   The Third Bridge, **Noonday** 3, December 1959, 70-82. [A7]

C 31   The Rain, **The New Yorker**, 23 April 1960, 40-43. [A8]

C 32   The Full Length Portrait, **The New Yorker**, 14 May 1960, 39-43. [A8]

C 33   A Coin With a Hole in It, **The New Yorker**, 4 June 1960 36-39. [A8] **The New Yorker** incorporated into this chapter of **Emblems of Conduct** some passages from "The Blond Bed," another chapter of the book, although the magazine publication preceded the book's publication.

C 34   The Man Who Could Not Come Into the House, **The New Yorker**, 30 July 1960, 21-24. [A8]

C 35   The Chifforobe, **The New Yorker**, 22 October 1960, 146-56. [A8]

C 36   Violence in Venice, **The Hasty Papers**, 1960, 34-38. This self-described "one-shot review," edited and published by the painter Alfred Leslie, in an oversized format also contained work by William Arrowsmith, John Ashbery, Gregory Corso, Allen Ginsberg, Jack Kerouac, Toby Olson, Joel Oppenheimer, Jean Paul Sartre, and James Schuyler, among others, so its bibliographical significance is considerable. Windham's autobiographical reminiscence about traveling from Venice to Sirmione with Truman Capote during the summer of 1948 is markedly different from Capote's version, titled "To Europe" in his **Local Color.**

C 37   Paolo, **Katholieke Illustratie** [Belgium],
        22 April 1961, 16-17 +19. [A7, B4, C27]

C 38   De Lening ["The Warm Country," trans-
        lated as "The Lending"], **Katholieke
        Illustratie** [Belgium], 22 June 1961, 16-
        19. [A7, C14]

C 39   Gentian, **The New Yorker**, 17 November
        1962, 53-58. [A8]

C 40   New Songs Will Be Misunderstood: I'm
        dancing with tears in my eyes, for the
        girl in my arms is a Jew . . . , **Kulchur**
        12, Winter 1963, 27-29. Windham's essay
        -- on prejudice in the South when he was
        growing up there -- is one in a series
        in this issue entitled "Rights: Some
        Personal Reactions"; other contributors
        include Leroi Jones, A. B. Spellman,
        Robert Williams, Gilbert Sorrentino, Ed
        Dorn, Joel Oppenheimer, and Denise
        Levertov.

C 41   Myopia, **The New Yorker**, 13 July 1963.
        [A8]

C 42   Letter to the Editor [about Stanley
        Kauffman's negative review of **Two
        People**], **New York Review of Books**, 9
        December 1965.

C 43   Letter to the Editor [about Stanley
        Kauffman's negative review of Truman
        Capote's **In Cold Blood**], **New Republic**,
        5 February 1966.

C 44   Letter to the Editor [about Windham's
        having ghost-written George Balanchine's
        notes on choreography, C12], **Spectator**
        [London], 11 March 1966.

C 45   "Joseph Cornell, December 24, 1903 --
        December 29, 1972: Events of the
        afternoon of August 15, 1955," **Village
        Voice**, 11 January 1973. Printed in
        tandem with a brief memoir of Cornell by
        Jonas Mekas, Windham's impressionistic
        narrative is actually a literal listing,

cast as events, to approximate in verbal
images some fantastic objects, collages,
and boxes he had seen during his visit
with Cornell.

C 46   Fame Kept Him Silent [an introduction to
"The Obelisk" by E. M. Forster], **Vogue**,
March 1973, 141.

C 47   Anne Ryan and Her Collages, **Art News**,
May 1974, 76-78.
Windham's original title for this
biographical essay, concentrating on
Ryan's work in collage, was "Anne Ryan:
A Hyacinth."

C 48   Letter to the Editor [about Dore
Ashton's <u>A Joseph Cornell Album</u>, Hilton
Kramer's review of it, and its
misrepresentations and errors], **New York
Times Book Review**, 2 February 1975.

C 49   [Comments and notes from] Tennessee
Williams' Letters to Donald Windham,
1940-1965, **Christopher Street** 2, October
1977, 11-12. [B6]

C 50   Letter to the Editor [about Robert
Brustein's negative review of **Tennessee
Williams' Letters to Donald Windham** and
Williams's letter in response to the
review], **New York Times Book Review**, 15
January 1978, 14.

C 51   Letter to the Editor [defending J. R.
Ackerley against slighting remarks by
Noel Annan in his review of P. N.
Furbank's biography of E. M. Forster],
Times [London] **Literary Supplement**, 14
April 1978.
This letter is quoted in **Ackerley** by
Peter Parker, p. 412. [D14]

C 52   Joseph Cornell's Unique Statement, **New
York Times**, 16 November 1980.
Windham wrote this memoir of the artist
in observation of the Cornell
retrospective exhibition at the Museum
of Modern Art, titling it "The Reward of

the Puzzle," after Cornell's own title for a series of collages, "Puzzle of the Reward." **The New York Times** changed that to the less appropriate "Joseph Cornell's Unique Statement."

C 53   Donald Windham Replies to Dotson Rader, **London Magazine** 20, February–March 1981, 80-88. In thirteen numbered paragraphs, Windham listed instances of defamatory and untrue statements and dishonest quotations in Dotson Rader's review of **Tennessee Williams' Letters to Donald Windham**, printed three years earlier in **London Magazine.** It was preceded by the "Statement in Open Court" of Counsel to the magazine's editor Alan Ross and the magazine as plaintiffs, acknowledging and apologizing in summary for the lies and misleading quotations in Rader's review. Rader was judged in default of appearance, being a citizen of the United States and out of the jurisdiction of the British Courts.

C 54   Letter to the Editor [protesting a Letter to the Editor written on behalf of **London Magazine**], [London] **Times Literary Supplement**, 10 April 1981, 409. Windham's letter refutes the claims of eight British writers [E121] regarding **London Magazine's** "settled defamation action not of its seeking" and possible bankruptcy as a result of the circumstances spelled out in C53, by pointing out that **London Magazine** had left him no choice but to sue since it refused to correct voluntarily the libelous statements in Rader's scurrilous review [E116].

C 55   Early Friends [selections from introduction and notes to **Tennessee Williams' Letters to Donald Windham**], **Tennessee Williams Review** 4, Spring 1983, 44-45. [B6]

C 56   Tennessee Williams: Fictions of a Lifetime [review of **Tennessee Williams:**

An Intimate Biography, by Dakin Williams and Shepherd Mead], Washington Post Book World, 14 April 1983, 3-4.

C 57   Tennessee Williams: Humpty-Dumpty Before, During, and After the Fall [review of The Kindness of Strangers, by Donald Spoto], Christopher Street 94, November 1984, 49-51. This collective title includes Sandy Campbell's review of Dotson Rader's book about Williams, The Cry of the Heart.

C 58   Introduction to "A Sage Conversation," by Augustus P. Longstreet, Christopher Street 100, May 1985, 54.
"A Sage Conversation," originally published in book form in Georgia Scenes in 1835, was here reprinted in a slightly abbreviated version.

C 59   The Hitchhiker, Christopher Street 101, June 1985, 30-34. [A3]
The text of the story occupies pp. 31 and 34; p. 30 is a reproduction of one of Paul Cadmus early portraits of Windham, and p. 33 is a facsimile of a holograph letter to Windham from Thomas Mann in praise of "The Hitchhiker."

C 60   My Side of the Matter [review of Capote by Gerald Clarke], Christopher Street 124, June 1988, 14-23.
More a reminiscence than a review, Windham's article was accompanied by reproductions of four photographs of Capote and himself taken by Sandy Campbell.

C 61   The Real Camino [review of Five O'Clock Angel: Tennessee Williams' Letters to Maria St. Just and Costly Performances: Tennessee Williams: The Last Stage, by Bruce Smith], New York Review of Books, 19 July 1990, 12+14.

D. Ephemera

D 1 **Fritz Bultman**, an untitled note about the painter on the verso of a deckle-edged, olive green card, 10.5 X 22.8 cm., printed in black; on recto: HUGO GALLERY / 26 East 55 . N.Y. 22 / [on left] opening may 19 / though may 31 - 1947 / [on right in heavy typeface] Fritz / Bultman

D 2 **Fritz Bultman**, a subsequent issue of D1 on lower third of a coated orange leaf, 43.X 19.0 cm., folded twice; top third: HUGO GALLERY / 26 EAST 55 STREET NEW YORK / FRITZ / BULTMAN / JANUARY 30 -- FEBRUARY 19 [1949]; middle third: reproduction of a Bultman painting; on coated peach verso: list of fourteen paintings

D 3 **Aviary**, an untitled note about Joseph Cornell on an ivory leaf printed in blue, folded once to make a brochure, 21.5 X 14.0 cm. [1] aviary / by / Joseph Cornell / December 1949 / [decoration] / Egan Gallery / 63 East 57 St., N.Y.C.; [2] note; [3] list of collages; [4, decoration]

D 4 **Ann Ryan Collages**, a note about the collagist in a pamphlet 20.5 X 20.3 cm., made of two folded and stapled

heavy white leaves. [1] ANNE RYAN
COLLAGES; [2] APRIL 24 -- MAY 11 [1963]
STABLE GALLERY, 33 E. 74 ST., NEW YORK;
[3] photograph of Anne Ryan; [4] PREVIEW
APRIL 24, 5-7; [5] A PERSONAL NOTE [by
Windham]; [6] untitled note by Gordon
Bailey Washburn; [7] list of museums
with Ryan works in their permanent
collections; [8] blank. Issued in a
blank envelope.

D 5   **Anne Ryan**, an untitled note about the
collagist in a coated white leaf french-
folded to 18.7 X 13.4 cm. [1] ANNE RYAN
/ (1889-1954) / COLLAGES / January 27 --
February 22, 1968 / Fishbach Gallery, 29
West 57th Street, New York, New York;
[2] note; [3] reproduction in full color
of a Ryan collage; [4] list of museums
with Ryan works in their permanent
collections and identification of the
collage reproduced in the brochure.
Issued in an envelope with gallery name
and address.

D 6   **My Father and Myself** by J. R. Ackerley,
an endorsement on the front flap of the
dust jacket of the American edition:
photographic cover of Ackerley and his
father printed in pale aqua with magenta
and orange lettering, Coward McCann,
1969.

D 7   ["The wonder of beauty . . ."], a
passage from **Emblems of Conduct** printed
on a cream card, 23.0 X 16.5 cm., 10
June 1974, issued by Robert M.
Willingham, Jr., signed by Windham and
numbered 1/5 through 5/5.

D 8   **Charles Henri Ford**, untitled note about
the photographer in a single-fold
brochure 14.7 X 21.6 cm., printed in
black on a coated white heavy leaf. [1]
CHARLES HENRI FORD / <u>Thirty Images from
Italy</u> / NOVEMBER 5 - 29, 1975 / CARLTON
GALLERY, 127 EAST 69 STREET, NEW YORK,
N.Y. 10021; [2] note, signed "Donald
Windham (<u>and Henry James</u>)" / four

photographs by Ford; [4] gallery name and address repeated. Issued in an envelope with gallery name and address. Windham alternated his sentences with sentences from **William Wetmore Story**, Henry James's biography of the nineteenth century sculptor.

D 9   ["I am unmarried but not unsettled"], a brief autobiographical note about Windham's interests, in **World Authors 1950-1970**, John Wakeman, editor, New York: H. W. Wilson, 1975, 1560.

D 10   ["I try to write about reality. . ."], Windham's brief commentary about his aims as a writer, in **Contemporary Novelists**, 2nd edition, James Vinson, editor, New York: St. Martin's Press, 1976, 1527.

D 11   **An Atlanta Christmas, 1930**, printed on a cream leaf french-folded to 17.8 X 12.8 cm. [1] AN / ATLANTA / CHRISTMAS, / 1930 [the foregoing in red, enclosed in a single-line green box] / text; [2-3] text, followed by [in red] "<u>Printed as a Christmas greeting for Richard Harwell with the permission of Donald Windham by The Stinehour Press, Lunenburg, Vermont</u>; [4] "The description of an Atlanta Christmas is an excerpt from Donald Windham's story "The Starless Air" in his **The Warm Country** (London: 1960). Mr. Windham says that his story describes a Christmas early in the Depression, probably 1930, but that the meal detailed is an amalgam of family Christmas dinners and could be based on any from 1925 to 1935." One hundred copies were printed in 1977, 50 unsigned; 25 signed first by Windham and then by Harwell; 25 signed first by Harwell and then by Windham.

D 12   **ERRATUM to footnote 2 on page 345: "The Art of Theatre V: Tennessee Williams" This interview with Tennessee Williams was reprinted from the <u>Paris Review</u>,**

number 81. The following correction to
footnote 2 appeared in <u>Paris Review</u>,
number 83. This 12.7 X 10.1 cm. white
card, issued by the University of
Mississippi Press, corrected Dotson
Rader's claim in the footnote that
Windham's libel suit against **London
Magazine** had been settled out of court.
It reviews the court's action and the
amount that the magazine's editor
claimed he was obliged to pay in court
costs, plaintiff's costs, and legal
fees. Although unsigned, the text of
the erratum is by Windham.

D 13   **Letters of Carl Van Vechten,** selected
and edited by Bruce Kellner, an
endorsement on the back of the dust
jacket: black cover with magenta and
half-tone lettering and a caricature of
Van Vechten in black and white and half-
tone by Ralph Barton, Yale University
Press, 1987. The endorsement was
reprinted in part in the fall 1990
Daedalus book sale catalog when the book
was remaindered.

D 14   **Ackerley: The Life of J. R. Ackerley** by
Peter Parker, an endorsement on the back
of the dust jacket: photographic cover
of Ackerley and his dog Queenie, printed
in lavender and cream over half-tone;
black, cream, grey, and wine lettering.
Farrar, Straus & Giroux, 1989. Windham's
letter to the [London] **Times Literary
Supplement** editor [C51] is reprinted in
Parker's biography, p. 412.

E. Criticism and Biography

1943

E 1   Peter Bellamy, "The Play," **Cleveland**
        [Ohio] **Union Leader**, 1 October.
        "Essentially a series of brilliant
        character sketches blended with over-
        tones of humor, tragedy, and Saroyan-
        esque poetic fancies, **You Touched Me**
        struck the reviewer as "verbose," with
        "patently artificial" dialogue, but
        "beautifully acted" by Carl Benton Reid,
        Reigh Walston, and Anne Pitoniak.

E 2   Omar Ranney, "Drama at Playhouse
        Promising," **Pasadena** [California] **Star
        News**, circa 10 November.
        You Touched Me -- a month after its
        tryout in Cleveland -- was just as the
        work of "young authors who write with
        considerable beauty and power of
        expression, . . . uncommonly adept at
        creating characters with down-to-earth,
        human qualities.

1945

E 3   "Dame," [review of **You Touched Me!**]
        Boston Globe, 19 September.
        A "hardworking, capable cast" added
        weight to a "conventional" drama,
        although the anonymous reviewer singled

out Montgomery Clift and Marianne
Stewart in the juvenile roles as
inadequate.

E 4   Lewis Nicol, [review of **You Touched
        Me!**], **New York Times,** 26 September.
        The reviewer judged the play "not
        entirely believable and "a step down"
        for Williams from **The Glass Menagerie.**
        It required "editing as well as
        cohesion" because it was "verbose and
        filled with lofty and long speeches."

E 5   John Chapman, "You Touched Me! This
        Season's First Competent, Amusing Play,"
        New York Herald Tribune, 26 September.
        You Touched Me! was "written by men who
        have a feeling for talk and character,
        . . . handsomely and carefully staged by
        [Guthrie McClintic] who knows that the
        theatre can be a place of illusion and
        charm." Chapman admired the performers
        -- notably Edmund Gwenn and Montgomery
        Clift -- and the humor that Williams and
        Windham had employed "lightly and
        deftly."

E 6   Susanne Donaldson, "Broadway Hit from
        Boys' High," **Atlanta Journal Magazine,**
        16 December.
        This interview with Windham supplied
        information about his background in
        Atlanta and the earlier tryouts for **You
        Touched Me!** Donaldson was writing for a
        wide popular audience, so the article
        was largely superficial.

1950

E 7   "The Dog Star," **Kirkus** 18, 1 March.
        Despite some unspecified "graphic,
        genuine values," the novel was "not for
        entertainment."

E 8   "Perceptive Study," **Syracuse** [New York]
        Post Standard, 22 April.
        The reviewer admired the "simple and
        discerning prose" in which Windham had
        written **The Dog Star,** the story of "an

irresponsible and reprehensible
idealist."

E 9   "Atlanta Slums and a Youth," **Augusta**
[Georgia] **Chronicle**, 23 April.
This indignant reviewer did not understand **The Dog Star**, found it hard to
follow, did not like it, and said so.

E 10   "Thomas Mann Sees Need for Anti-
Fascism," **New York Herald Tribune**, 29
April.
In an interview before his departure for
Europe to celebrate his 75th birthday,
Mann singled out **The Dog Star** from
recent American novels for praise, as
"simple, natural, and strong."

E 11   Warren Leslie, "Novelette Form Poses
Problem," **Dallas** [Texas] **Times-Herald**,
30 April.
Using his review of **The Dog Star** as a
platform to condemn the novella as "an
illegitimate literary form," Leslie then
accused Windham of having "rewritten
several books of James T. Farrell among
others without con-spicuous success." As
The Dog Star is not a novella either in
form or length (nor are Farrell's
novels), Leslie's dismissal of it as
"strong, ordered, well-mannered, and
without much reason to be" is a peculiar
assessment.

E 12   Hilda Noel Schroetter, "Boy's Tragedy,"
Richmond [Virginia] **Dispatch**, 30 April.
Schroetter admired the "sheer poetry"
and "stark beauty" in **The Dog Star**, a
novel "too clear not to be compelling."

E 13   "The Dog Star," **The New Yorker**, 6 May,
117.
"The uniform pettiness of Mr. Windham's
characters scarcely justifies his spare,
intense style."

E 14   Hubert Creekmore, "Adolescent, Doomed,"
New York Times Book Review, 7 May, 20.
In this less cursory review than those

written earlier for **The Dog Star**,
Creekmore referred to "many admirable
qualities [of] serious conception,
complex and stimulating overtones, neat
descriptions and fine execution which
have been lacking in most fiction of the
last few years." He called attention to
the "clinical barrenness" of the writing
that risked "in not making the hero
loveable."

E 15   "Potpourri," **Atlantic Monthly**, May, 87.
An "ably written," "unpretentious," and
"perceptive study of twisted idealism,"
The Dog Star was admired by the reviewer
for its "real understanding and compassion" for the central character and his
"touch little world. . . ."

E 16   C. M. Brown, "The Dog Star," **Saturday
Review of Literature**, 24 June, 30.
"An acute document on that slovenly
segment of society at the moment associated with the South. Parched, dusty,
and more often than not avoidably
intimate."

E 17   J. J. Maloney, "The Dog Star," **New York
Herald Tribune Book Review**, 16 July, 10.
The reviewer felt no compassion for the
protagonist who lacked "the spark of
warmth which one expects to find in
every boy, no matter how delinquent."
Windham wrote "extremely well," he con-
ceded, wishing that his "undoubted
talent had been spent in portraying a
character about whom one could care more
than one cares about Blackie."

E 18   Katherine Gauss Jackson, "Books in
Brief," **Harper's Magazine**, July.
The reviewer questioned the authenticity
of the point of view of a fifteen year
old, especially if it was articulate;
the "unbearably bleak" action; the
"high-flown language" used to express
"warped aspirations," and the lack of "a
creative spark of compassion which might
give life to dreary characters." She

remarked, however, on Windham's
"sensitive and perceptive mind."

1951

E 19   Warren Abbott, Jr., "Case Worker's Novel
of Cruel Adolescent, **Chicago Tribune**, 1
January.
Noting that Theodore Dreiser had been
condemned for writing about non-
entities, Abbott noted that **The Dog Star**
was "entirely serious and, on serious
ground, entirely interesting," even if
it "plumbs gutters even lower than
Dreiser's" in "distilled paragraphs,
gaunt and spare."

E 20   "Recent Novels," **Irish Times**, 22 September.
The Dog Star was judged "an efficient
and unpretentious parable which holds
the stock conclusions on the competing
claims of heredity and environment; and
the braggadocio of the central character
and his friends is unpleasantly lifelike."

E 21   Simon Raven, "New Novels," **The Listener**,
27 September.
The Dog Star had the "eternal validity
of legend: it delineates a truth that
is too powerful to be a cliche against a
background that is too mean to be anything else."

E 22   John Richardson, "New Novels," **New
Statesman**, 6 October.
The Dog Star, compared the Nathanael
West's **The Day of the Locust**, struck the
reviewer as "almost genteel" and characteristic of much post-war American
fiction and painting. Like Gore Vidal,
Truman Capote, and Tennessee Williams,
Windham used the "props and . . .
cliches of 'Symbolic Realism,'" but the
novel was meaningless though "unusually
well written. . . ."

E 23   L. P. Hartley, "The New Barsetshire,"

[London] **Sunday Times**, 7 October.
Windham's "unpleasant but well-written
story" about "sex-mad, paranoiac teen-
agers" insisted on "the destructive,
lone-wolf element that is seldom absent
from the masculine make-up." Moreover,
Hartley found the "allegorical aspects
insufficiently made out" in **The Dog
Star**.

1953

E 24   "Tennessee Williams Directs 'Starless'
at Playhouse," **Houston Press**, 8 May.
Windham's dramatization of his story
"The Starless Air" offered "the fullest
emotional experience Houston audiences
have had an opportunity to seek
recently," including two of Tennessee
Williams's plays. Each of the fifteen
characters, however, seemed to have his
own scene, so that the play was "lifelike but diffused, . . . scattering its
shots to point morals. . . ."

E 25   Paul Hochuli, "Playhouse Premieres
'Starless Air,' and It Could Do With a
Bit of Fixing," **Houston Press**, 14 May.
Although the reviewer thought Windham
had "the ingredients for a good play,"
"The Starless Air" began "like a house
afire, but seems to run out of fuel as
it progresses." The reviewer pointed
out a balance of "clever lines and dull
lines," an "insecure cast," and the need
for "a hellfire rehearsal."

1960

E 26   "The Hero Continues," [London] **Daily
Telegraph**, 29 April.
The anonymous reviewer thought Windham
used words "as a highly mechanical brain
might -- and his cool detachment" led to
the "unnerving reality of a very bad
dream in a padded cell."

E 27   Paul West, "New Novels," **New Statesman**
59, 30 April, 643.

There were "masterly changes of pace" in
The Hero Continues, but they were
"rather too knowing, as if [the pro-
tagonist] Denis Freeman himself had
ghosted parts of it."

E 28   Storm Jameson, "The Penalties of Success," [London] **Sunday Times**, 1 May. An
"immensely talented" writer, Windham was
"a master of visual detail." **The Hero
Continues** "blinds with excess of light,"
however, "at moments when he should be
as plain as he is vivid."

E 29   Oswell Blakeston," New Novels," **Time and
Tide** 517, 7 May, 520.
The protagonist in **The Hero Continues**
"pretends that he following some higher
destiny of renunciation . . . or, more
smugly, that he working his way through
the disasters which 'make writing necessary,'" although the reviewer thought
Windham's "astringency . . . puts an
edge on the literary parties and the
stabbing, strangulating, mutilating but
otherwise encouraging practices of
Broadway impresarios."

E 30   Malcolm Bradbury, "New Novels," **Punch**,
11 May, 667.
Despite "great imaginative deftness" and
"something of Scott Fitzgerald's piti-
less eye," the reviewer thought Windham's "images can become too strong."

E 31   "The Hero Continues," [London] **Times
Literary Supplement**, 27 May, 333.
Recalling the careers of F. Scott Fitzgerald, Thomas Wolfe and others, the
reviewer did not doubt Windham's factual
veracity but questioned "the lack of
curiosity about the stony ground of a
culture in which talents spring up and
wither away."

E 32   R. H. Donahugh, "The Hero Continues,
Library Journal 85, August, 2819.
"Extremely episodic, there is in this
book only the most meager attempt at

establishing any background or character. Some of the dialogue is fairly
amusing. . . . Perhaps it is symbolic;
maybe it is a joke. To this reviewer it
is merely dull and meaningless. Not for
libraries."

E 33   Gene Baro, "The Hero Continues," **New
York Herald Tribune Book Review**, 18
September, 6.
Windham's hero continued as "the victim
of his own fulfillment, the god that
must die in the world to be reborn in
his work," a "serious theme," handled
with "taste and distinction."

E 34   E. M. Forster, "Introduction" to **The
Warm Country** by Donald Windham. London:
Rupert Hart-Davis.
Forster offered to write this warm
endorsement of Windham's stories [A7].
In it he observed that the most im-
portant thing about the writer was his
belief in "warmth": "He knows that
human beings are not statues but contain
flesh and blood and a heart, and he
believes that creatures so constituted
must contact one another or they will
decay." Also, the introduction included
line sufficiently memorable to have been
quoted more often than any other about
Donald Windham: "Mr Windham, I
understand, has never learnt literature;
he merely produces it."

E 35   "New Fiction," [London] **Daily Times**, 8
December.
The stories in **The Warm Country** struck
the reviewer as "mere adumbrations of a
situation, like notes for something
somewhat longer," but the prose was
"suave," with "a soft, almost feminine
impression."

E 36   Ronald Bryden, "Bearing Gifts," **Spectator**, 9 December.
The stories in **The Warm Country** were
about "vaguely omnious relationships"
and "Gothic hints about the dark,

frightening places where love can lead";
the reviewer averred he "wouldn't leave
them under a Christmas tree without a
plain wrapper."

E 37   Jeremy Brooks, "The Warm Country,"
[Manchester] **Guardian** 9 December, 7.
"One might easily overlook the elusive
qualities that lie beneath the quiet,
matter-of-fact surface of these stories.
They make little immediate impact; but
long after one has laid them aside their
warmly human comments reverberate in
one's mind like memories called up by a
forgotten scent encountered unexpectedly
in a foreign land."

E 38   Penelope Mortimer, "Away From It All,"
[London] **Sunday Times**, 18 December.
The stories in **The Warm Country** "slide
sideways on to life, giving it . . . no
more than a stealthy glance," but the
reviewer thought Windham "undoubtedly
far and way the most serious and
talented writer on this Sunday's list,"
which included Robert Nathan, Margaret
Culkin, Josephine Blumenfeld, and Jack
Schaefer.

E 39   Sue Brown Sterne, "Guggenheim Fellow
Began Playwriting in Atlanta High
School," [Atlanta] **Sunday Journal**, 18
December.
Windham's interviewer tended to gush in
language more suitable for a fan magazine, but she included some biographical
information regarding Windham's early
attempts at drama and his brief art
instruction at Georgia Tech.

E 40   Richard Whittington, "Shows Small Insight into Warm Country," **Baton Rouge**
[Louisiana] **Sunday Advocate**, 23
December.
This shrill response canceled itself out
through its own hysteria. The reviewer
objected to love's being realized only
in "perverted relationships among
sailors, prostitutes, artists, and

Negroes," since Windham did not demonstrate "the craftsmanship necessary to
transform such a convention into
rewarding literature. He condemned "The
Starless Air" as "a seedy southern version of Joyce's "The Dead," and Windham
himself because "he writes of the
Southern character with all the insight
of a British sailor passing through
Georgia on a bus."

E 41   Robin Denniston, "Short and Not So
Short," **Time and Tide**, 24 December.
The stories in **The Warm Country** struck
the reviewer as "difficult to appreciate
because the point . . . is so firmly
lodged in the atmosphere . . . that
there seems little reason for them to
end or begin." Since he contended that
all of the stories took place in America, it is unlikely that he read the
book through.

E 42   Malcolm Bradbury, "New Fiction," **Punch**,
28 December, 950.
An "indirection in presentation" and a
"concern to present the nuances and
subtleties of human contact in everyday
situations" pervade the stories in **The
Warm Country**, but Bradbury had reservations about what he thought was
usually called a "poetic" effect. He
did not doubt Windham's "sensitivity or
his skill," but he would have preferred
"considered, willed action" to "ordinary
people . . . made to expose their actions, their loneliness, the flickering
nature of their affections, the slight-
ness of their love."

1962

E 43   "The Warm Country," **Kirkus**, 11 April.
Windham's collection of short stories
"disobeys every one of the recipes
concocted by the scullery maids of
saleable fiction and the engineers who
reduce plot structure to ell-shaped
curves." He singled out "Paolo" as

"flawless" and "classic."

E 44   Charles Poore, "Books of the Times," **New York Times**, 12 April.
The Warm Country lived up to the praise in E. M. Forster's preface, the work of "a virtuoso writer . . . . who reverses and expands . . . at will Emerson's quiet desperation" and Lord Acton's observation that "power corrupts" with a "noisy desperation, corrupted by too little power." Poore praised particularly the "unsparing clarity" of "The Starless Air."

E 45   "Uphappy Love Explored in All Its Vagaries," **Buffalo** [New York] **Evening News**, 14 April.
Comparing but not claiming equality for the stories in **The Warm Country** with those of Joyce, Sherwood Anderson, and Chekhov, the reviewer called Windham "the laureate of frustration and acceptance rather than of ecstasy and fruition." His forte was "to make the inarticulate articulate through the imaged situation, to carve and whittle moments of epiphany along life's human grain. . . ."

E 46   T. E. Adams, "Believably Human Beings Drawn With Honesty and Compassion," **Louisville** [Kentucky] **Courier Journal**, 15 April.
In **The Warm Country** Adams found "honesty and compassion" often missing in fiction and a "distinct impression that his stories are worth re-reading, worth thinking more about."

E 47   J. N., "The Warm Country," **New York Herald Tribune Books**, 15 April, 7.
"Donald Windham eschews most of the conventional blandishments of fiction. His is the art of the small incident scrupulously explored in precise, grave and cultivated prose. . . . Those with no particular taste for literary chamber music may find that 'The Warm Country'

yields only sparse rewards. Nevertheless, several of these stories speak
strongly. . . . The book as a whole
gives the impression of being lifelike
rather than lively."

E 48   George Freedley, "Windham Expert at
Short Story," **New York Morning
Telegraph**, 24 April.
At a time when many writers seemed bent
on "maudlin self-revelation . . . with
intention to shock," Freedley admired
Windham's "refreshing restraint" and
called him "a genuine artist and a master of the short story form."

E 49   Dennis Powers, "The Warm Country is
Uneven Terrain," **Oakland** [California]
Tribune, 26 April.
Two of Windham's stories were "downright
mediocre" and two or three were "notably
successful." Powers thought Windham
lacked what the majority of reviewers
praised: "a real flow of language, an
excellence of expression to match the
intelligence and insight of the observation."

E 50   C. E. Moore, "Ex-Atlantan's Book Fails
Its Characters," **Atlanta Journal**, 29
April.
Windham's "knowledge of human physiology
didn't quite make its way into the
beings he has drawn in this thin volume"
who were "giddy shells striking poses
and lisping gush." Moore based his
assessment on a single story in **The Warm
Country**, concluding, "My, my."

E 51   Jeremy Larner, "The Warm Country," **New
York Times Book Review**, 13 May.
"Donald Windham's sense of balance is
infallible; there is not a single bad
story or spoiled story in the book.
Everything is handled with a purity of
language and emotion that moves the
reader directly and without distractions
to the unique anguish of each story's
hero. Words are used carefully, but

transparently, so that they never get
between the reader and what Windham
wants him to care about. From the first
word the reader believes and trusts and
cares. . . . In their relentless honesty, pessimism, and refusal to detach
individuals from the forces that create
and destroy them, the stories of 'The
Warm Country' contrast sharply with the
prevalent tendency to use the short
story as a means of exploring and glor-
ifying the exotic possibilities of
individualism. Donald Windham . . . is
an uncommon, unfashionable writer,
without the slightest trace of slick,
and only his downright power will gain
him the eventual audience he deserves."

E 52   Joseph LeSeur, "Individuals All," **Vil-
         lage Voice**, 23 June.
         Unlike most Southern writers, Windham
         called "no attention to style," had "no
         mannerisms," and was "subtle but not
         abstruse." In LeSeur's view Windham's
         stories in **The Warm Country** were "too
         honest; and that's a quality critics and
         readers seem not to be interested in
         these days."

E 53   Dorothy Parker, "The Warm Country,"
         Esquire, June.
         Drawing attention to E. M. Forster's
         introduction, Parker called the stories
         in **The Warm Country** "warm and thoughtful
         and discerning," but she wished she had
         been more deeply impressed by them.

                        1964

E 54   Henry Butler, "The Sacrifices to Social
         Pressure," **Indianapolis Times**, 19
         January.
         The reviewer addressed his reader
         directly about **Emblems of Conduct:** "a
         book to remind you of how much you've
         learned to forget about your childhood
         and how much you've lost by so learn-
         ing." He admired Windham's style,
         "remarkable for its simplicity and

allusiveness" and its "integrity."

E 55   John Alden Long, "Voyage and Return,"
Christian Science Monitor, 23 January,
5.
Emblems of Conduct offered Long evidence
of Windham's "increasingly significant
writings" and his "growth of self-aware-
ness."

E 56   Alan Pryce-Jones, "A Childhood in
Atlanta," **New York Herald Tribune**, 23
January.
"Mr. Windham works over his material
like a careful water-color artist,
holding a delicate brush and a palette
of pale sunlit intensity," free of
sentimentality and nostalgia. Pryce-
Jones found **Emblems of Conduct** especially winning because it was "solidly
founded on happiness," despite the
unhappiness it sometimes reflected. He
particularly admired the later chapters
"where childhood is shading away into
adolescence."

E 57   Frank Daniel, "Ex-Atlantan Writes of a
Grand Childhood," **Atlanta Constitution
and Journal**, 26 January.
Despite the odd adjective in his title,
Daniel found **Emblems of Conduct** "extraordinarily fine and moving," although he
thought "the later chapters lost some of
the sparkle and spontaniety."

E 58   Jeanne Lopez, "Emblems of Conduct,"
Library Journal 89, 1 February.
Lopez dismissed Windham's memoir as the
"raw material for previously published
stories" and thought the writing uneven
with "spots of dull detail and obvious
padding." Moreover, she contended that
"an author writing his life in order to
understand himself is aiming for a one-
man public."

E 59   Morley Driver, "Boyhood," **Detroit Free
Press**, 2 February.
Identifying **Emblems of Conduct** as a
"novel," Driver observed that the "whole

emotional climate of childhood is set
forth in an unemotional way and sorts
itself out with painful economy." He
compared Windham with James Agee as "a
young writer of extraordinary ability
and subtlety."

E 60   Victor P. Hass, "Luminous Fragment of
American Life," **Chicago Tribune**, 2
February.
Noting that it is easier to identify
with the lives of little people rather
than big ones, Hass called **Emblems of
Conduct** "an excellent book, a gentle
book, an often rich and revealing book
of one boy in a particular time and
place," and "a fine portrait of middle
class American life."

E 61   Thomas Goldthwaire, "Vivid Memories
Aided By Muse of Childhood,"
Indianapolis Star, 2 February.
Windham's "lucid and natural" prose
effected "the happy blend of a child's
disturbingly correct evaluation of an
immense environment, coupled with a
talented author's restraint in mature
objectivity. The first reviewer to
allude even elliptically to the homosexuality in **Emblems of Conduct**, Goldthwaire would have preferred to have
been "spared the details of [Windham's]
anxieties, his rather psycho-physical
[sic] friends. . . . Perhaps Windham
will live to regret those painful chapters wherein his growing pains are
recorded with such burdening intro-
spection." Nevertheless, he assessed
the book as the work of "an unashamedly
honest man."

E 62   Eleanor Perry, "Ah youth, or looking
back in langour," **Book Week**, 16 February, 5.
In this joint review of a book about
which she was less enthusiastic than
about **Emblems of Conduct**, Perry offered
her private test for what made a good
book: "a certain kind of slowed-down

reading because what is on the page
evokes so many memories, stirs up so
many feelings and thoughts. It is as if
the writer's narrative is a paper trail
laid down in a forest. One keeps track
of it constantly but at the same time is
vividly aware of the shape of trees,
sunlight and shadows, the flight of
birds. One arrives at the end of this
book not breathless but enriched."
Emblems of Conduct, and therefore Windham himself possessed "that all too rare
virtue these days -- taste," sensing
what to omit and relating "the emotions
of growing up so perceptively that one
is forced to look backwards into one's
own life and agree with him: yes, I
felt that too, that's exactly how it
was."

E 63   Ralph McGill, "Growing Up in Georgia,"
New York Times Book Review, 12 April,
18.
Deliberately truncated by the editors,
according to its author, this long-
delayed review praised **Emblems of
Conduct** as "an extraordinarily well
written book. . . . Here is a childhood
written with such integrity and a feeling of fidelity in time and place that
not merely Southerners will feel a sense
of recognition, but all others as well."
In McGill's view, Windham was "a writer
of genuine talent with a fine ear for
conversation and eye for detail."

E 64   Robert McAdams, "New Short Stories," **New
York Review of Books** 2, 30 April, 10.
Lumping it with some works of fiction,
McAdams seems not to have grasped that
Emblems of Conduct was an autobiography.
He described it as "a slight, careful
book . . . of charming little sketches"
but gave no indication that he had read
even the dust jacket.

1965

E 65   Elizabeth Jennings, "The Nova Mob," **The**

Spectator, 8 July, 202.
In a review including assessments of
William Burroughs's **Nova Express** and
other new novels, Jennings called **Two
People** "a study of the subtleties of
<u>simpatica</u> and of the city of Rome
itself," and Windham's treatment of his
subject "delicate and reticent."

E 66   Theodore O'Leary, "The More That's
Forbidden The More is Allowed," **Kansas
City Star**, 11 July.
"An immaculate book" whose "strength is
not its incipiently sensational subject," **Two People** stressed instead its
two cultures with what the reviewer
called Windham's "utmost discretion."

E 67   Mario Soldati, "Un amico straniero che
ci vede come siamo," **Il Giorno**, 13 July.
Windham's translation, "A Friendly
Foreigner Who Sees Us As We Are" notes
in detail that the title, **Two People** is
"untranslatable in Italian because it
can and here does mean at the same time
'Two Individuals' or 'Two National-
ities,' and not only the meaning of the
title but the inspiration of the novel
lies exactly in this ambivalence."
Soldati urged an Italian translation of
the novel because it would have "a fas-
cinating appeal" for Italians: "that of
suddenly discovering our own images,
which seem all the more real in the
limpid mirror of the prose of a foreign
writer who sees us as we are, even
though he loves us and judges with the
greatest charity." The novel, though
"affection as it is, hurts" because it
pointed out an essential hypocrisy in
Italian mores. Soldati's review was as
much a negative assessment of "the
carnal, anti-historical, anti-social
character of the Roman community" as it
was a positive assessment of **Two People.**

E 68   Tom Schlesinger, "'Two People' Classic
Only for Dullness," **Virginian Pilot**, 25
July.

This negative review of the dust jacket
endorsements by Tennessee Williams,
Truman Capote, and Luigi Barzini ignored
Windham's "trifling account peopled with
. . . so-what characters. . . ."

E 69   Heather Ross Miller, "Windham Misses on
Plot, People," **Charlotte** [North
Carolina] **Observer**, 1 August.
The reviewer was not only antagonistic
toward **Two People** but angry: ". . . a
series of neurotic dream-experiences,
. . . a pablum-tasting, heart-twanging,
confessional-type packet of nonsense
that lopes along like a blind beggar
asking for pity and perchance a few
coppers, . . . an unripened book plucked
before its time." The treatment of Rome,
which virtually every other reviewer
praised without qualification, she found
"colorless."

E 70   Dennis Powers, "The Roman Spring of Two
Lost Souls," **Focus Oakland** [California],
5 August.
"The writing is fine in its simplicity,
effective in its understatement. With
skill and restraint, Windham tells us
all we need to know about Forrest and
Marcello [in **Two People**] and their relationship. . . . Without being pretentious, Windham makes us aware that this
isn't a sordid tale of stolen moments,
but a story about two people helping
each other through a bad time in their
lives."

E 71   Eleanor Perry, "When in Rome, be careful," **Book Week**, 8 August.
Perry dismissed comparisons between **Two
People** and Thomas Mann's **Death in
Venice**, despite some obvious parallels,
and she wondered why "a talented and
skilful writer" of "remarkable talent"
bothered to write the novel.

E 72   Frank Daniel, "When in Rome, Who's to
Blame?" **Atlanta Journal**, 8 August.
Charles Jackson's **The Fall of Valor**,

also a novel about homosexuality, was
marred by "half-convincing moralizing,"
but **Two People** treated the same theme
with "a great deal of poetic flair,
. . . frankness and a special charm" and
a "tincture of romantic special pleading." Daniel managed this fulsome review
without mentioning that the teenager involved in the love affair was a boy.

E 73   Ann Fair Dodson, "As Strangers Meet in
Rome," [Springfield, Missouri] **Sunday
News and Leader**, 8 August.
The central "theme and thesis" of Windham's novel was the city of Rome itself
rather than its plot. **Two People**
"inspires compassion and understanding
-- where condemnation must surely have
followed the slightest slip of his pen."

E 74   Eliot Fremont-Smith, "An Academic
Wheeze, a Roman Interlude," **New York
Times**, 10 August, 65.
In a joint review, equally unkind to a
novel by G. B. Harrison, Fremont-Smith
dismissed **Two People** as "a vapid boy-
meets-boy affair." Windham, he allowed,
was "a gifted, quiet writer," but this
"aenemic" and "pretentious" novel was
"so devoid of relevancy that it may, to
some, seem art."

E 75   Jack F. Bernard, "Two People," **Best
Sellers**, 15 August, 211.
Disparaging Gore Vidal's having made of
the subject a problem "sensational with
angst and suicide to solve it, the
reviewer thought **Two People** had made
some advancement. Despite its
"stylistic and realistic brilliance,
humor, and intelligence," the novel left
him unsatisfied, although he admired it
"for its complete lack of vulgarity and
the tasteful restraint" in treating "an
unconventional subject."

E 76   "Sex in Fiction," [Madison, Wisconsin]
Capital Times, 20 August.
Two People was notable for its "per-

ceptive view of the Anglo-Saxon
character and the Latin in juxta-
position"; moreover, Windham's
"treatment of a story that would have
raised hackles a quarter of a century
ago" struck the reviewer positively:
"His novel is thoroughly modern, his
manner casual, his perspective sane."

E 77   Eleanor R. Mayo, "A Middle-Age Marriage
on the Rocks," [Cleveland, Ohio] **Plain
Dealer**, 29 August.
This angry reviewer found **Two People** "so
hopelessly flaccid it oozes like a Dali
watch," although her moral rather than
her aesthetic outrage seems to have
accounted for her response.

E 78   Martin Levin, "A Reader's Report," **New
York Times Book Review**, 29 August, 23.
Objecting to Windham's having allowed an
"emotionally retarded" Forrest to "brood
over his protege, in sentimental rumina-
tions that would cloy a love affair
between even the opposite sexes," Levin
betrayed his own prejudices through the
seemingly innocent but nevertheless
judgmental "even." Nor did he
strengthen his case in adding, "Hey,
remember them?" The notice was not only
mean-spirited but homophobic.

E 79   Hilton Kramer, "Queer Affirmations," **New
Leader** 48, 30 August.
After a grudging admission that "the
time is certainly ripe" for a "period of
queer affirmation," Kramer then regarded
"the prospect of a homosexual literature
written to the strains of hearts and
flowers with something less than joy."
As a novel "designed to reassure us that
queers are, after all, firm supporters
of home and hearth," **Two People** was
"probably too discreet for "a public
grown used to gamier fare," but it
pointed "a direction that others are
sure to follow." Windham's "tenuous
little fable is pederasty without tears
-- a homosexual romance, replete with

clean linen and sunlit views of Rome,
that raises no painful questions,
acquits its principals of all but the
tenderest motives, absolves them of all
guilt, and restores them, morally
intact, to the banalities of bourgeois
respectability." Throughout, Kramer
betrays his bias through snide asides
more often than through close attention
to the content of the novel.

E 80   Edith Schumaker, "Two People," **Library
        Journal** 90, August, 3313.
        The novel would require "discreet
        handling as many readers do not recog-
        nize the problems of homosexuality,"
        although the reviewer remarked Windham's
        "sensitivity and carefully chosen
        words."

E 81   Herbert Kubly, "Greek Love on the Span-
        ish Steps," **Saturday Review** 48, 11
        September, 43.
        Kubly recommended **Two People** for being
        "straight-forward," "unpretentious," and
        "devoid of prurient titillation,"
        although he thought Windham disappoint-
        ingly circumspect in his delineation of
        its subject.

E 82   "Two People," **Time**, 17 September,
        140+145.
        Using Windham's "perceptive,
        unsensational" novel as his model, the
        reviewer employed **Two People** to illus-
        trate a broader-ranging essay about
        distractions becoming obsessions and the
        arc linking sex and money.

E 83   Robert J. Kaller, "Argument for Evil,"
        Monterey Peninsula [California] **Herald**,
        19 September.
        In this strange attack, more notable for
        its alarming homophobia than for its
        literary perception, Kaller criticized
        the publication of **Two People** rather
        than the "merely dull" novel itself.
        "The alarm it sounds" indicated that
        "our society has gradually had its

fabric weakened to the point where it begins to see first a lack of threat and then positive virtues in such relationships" as the one between Forrest and Marcello, not only "perverse" but "a serious social evil." Condoning such evil, Kaller contended, we would become "tainted by it, and our communications media have already begun to show the inroads." Reading **Two People** was "an experience to make one's spiritual skin crawl."

E 84   Stanley Kauffman, "Queer Lives," **New York Review of Books** 5, 11 November, 32. Moral paranoia seems to have accounted for this scathing dismissal of **Midnight Cowboy** by James Leo Herlihy and **Slowly by Thy Hand Unfulfilled** by Romulus Linney as well as of **Two People**. Literary criticism was absent at least in Kauffman's unsupported generalizations about Windham's "cardboard prose with characters to match" and "absurd comments" about sexuality and friendship.

E 85   Gilbert Maxwell, **Tennessee Williams and Friends**, Cleveland: World Publishing Company, 47-49, 52-53, 57-60. This narrative includes a sporadic account of Windham's early associations with Williams.

1966

E 86   Robert Baldick, "Creatures of the New York Jungle," [London] **Daily Telegraph**, 10 February. In **Two People**, Windham conveyed to the reviewer "the special moral atmosphere" of Rome, but the relationship between Forrest and Marcello was treated with such "timorous delicacy" that it never served as "the watershed . . . it is obviously meant to be."

E 87   Ken Gray, "Aspects of Radicalism," **Irish Times**, 12 February.

Two People was "a sincere attempt to
cast the light of tolerant understanding
upon a relationship which most look upon
as unnatural, abhorrent and even
criminal," but the reviewer could not
share Windham's "worldly-wise air of
detachment from the moral implications"
of an affair that was "grossly
undignified and humiliating."

E 88   P. N. Furbank "A Hopeless Case,"
Observer, 13 February.
Later to become E. M. Forster's
biographer, Furbank found Windham's
"small theme . . . expertly handled" but
described the plot of **Two People** as "an
escape route to comfort."

E 89   Michael Ratcliffe, "Current Fiction,"
[London] **Sunday Times**, 13 February.
"Something is being said [in **Two People**]
about the absence of strong love and
affection, and the sense of uncompleted
gestures, of risked half-truths is
marvellously done; but the real pleasure
of the book lies in the writing itself.
Mr Windham deploys a fairly simple
Latinate vocabulary in sentences of an
almost baroque complexity, the best of
which is precisely calculated as to the
exact moral and syntactical weight that
each word has to bear. Thus he manages
to be both sensible and absorbing."

E 90   "Two People," [London] **Times Literary
Supplement**, 17 February.
The reviewer assessed the "cool, flat
manner" and "lucid and calm" prose as
"misleading" because "perhaps too much
is left unsaid" in **Two People**, although
it was "a decent, brave book. . . ."

E 91   Julie Tisdallon, "A Roman Delicacy,"
Books and Bookmen, March.
Concentrating on the homosexuality in
Two People, the reviewer thought the
plot was "therefore extraneous," since
love without "significance" was only "a
passing fancy." Windham showed what she

termed "admirable taste, and a wonder-
fully light touch," best when "simple"
and worst when "enigmatic," and "always
most effective when he says least." As
he said least more often than not, her
observation was a compliment, she
averred.

1974

E 92   Sandy Campbell, **B, Twenty-nine Letters
from Cocoanut Grove**, Verona: Stamperia
Valdonega, 2 July.
This collection of Campbell's letters to
Windham, written in January and February
1956, was published in an edition of 300
copies. Largely devoted to an account
of the rehearsals and production of a
revival of Tennessee Williams's **A
Streetcar Named Desire**, they contain
scattered references to Windham; Campbell's
"Foreword" accounts for further
biographical information during the period
1943-1956.

1975

E 93   "Donald Windham," **World Authors, 1950-
1970, A Companion Volume to Twentieth
Century Authors,** John Wakeman, Editor.
New York: H. W. Wilson, 1560-61.
This biographical entry accounts for
Windham's work through 1965 and, by way
of a brief statement he prepared for
inclusion, some indication of his
personal interests. [D9].

E 94   **E. M. Forster's Letters to Donald
Windham**, Donald Windham, Editor. Verona:
Stamperia Valdonega.
Published privately by Sandy Campbell,
Forster's letters contain careful
assessments, affectionate but objective,
of Windham's writing; they account, too,
for the progress of the friendship
between them. [B5]

1976

E 95   **The Ackerley Letters**, Neville Bray-
         brooke, Editor. New York: Harcourt
         Brace Jovanovich.
         This selection contains five letters to
         Windham and Sandy Campbell, with refer-
         ences to Windham in letters to
         others.

E 96   Dale K. Doepke, "Donald Windham,"
         Contemporary Novelists, 2nd edition,
         James Vinson, Editor, D. L. Kirk-
         patrick, Associate Editor. New York: St.
         Martin's Press, 1526-28.
         Doepke's brief criticism of Windham's
         work through 1965 includes a statement
         Windham prepared for inclusion about his
         aims as a writer. [D10].

E 97   **Tennessee Williams' Letters to Donald
         Windham, 1940-65**, Donald Windham,
         Editor. Verona: Stamperia Valdonega.
         First published privately by Sandy
         Campbell in a limited edition, and
         subsequently in a trade edition, Wil-
         liams's letters contain a running
         biographical account of his associations
         with Windham, both personal and
         professional. [B6]

E 98   Paul Bailey, "Confessing Loudly,"
         [London] **Times Literary Supplement**, 17
         December, 1576.
         In this joint review of Tennessee
         Williams's **Memoirs** and **Tennessee
         Williams' Letters to Donald Windham
         1940-65**, Bailey dismissed Williams's
         "shamefully badly written book" as
         "studied cuteness" because "of all
         bores, the sexual boaster is probably
         the most insufferable." Williams's early
         letters, however, were "wonderfully
         fresh and lively" since they were "free
         from paranoia" and Windham's running
         commentary explained "with real
         affection why he, and many others, was
         won over by the young charmer from the
         South. He also explains, with an
         accumulating sadness, why their once

perfect friendship was allowed to fade
away."

1977

E 99   "Tennessee Williams' Letters to Donald
Windham, 1940-1965," **Publisher's Weekly**
212, 8 August, 60.
This review and subsequent ones were
based on the trade edition of the book,
issued with slight revisions, by Holt,
Rinehart, and Winston: "The great value
of Windham's assemblage of these
letters, which diminished in frequency
as the years passed, is not so much what
they reveal of the playwright's celebrated sex life (the 'Memoirs' did
that), but what they show of his attitude toward his work and his relationships with others. Windham's informative commentary puts it all into perspective in what at times becomes almost
a mini-biography."

E 100   "Tanaquil," **Publisher's Weekly**, 213, 22
August, 6.
A novel marked by "seamlessness" and
"quiet realism," **Tanaquil** offered a
"rather subtle depiction of sensual
awakening" in prose that was "mild but
distinctive."

E 101   L. E. Bone, "Tennessee Williams' Letters
to Donald Windham, 1940-1965," **Library
Journal** 102, 15 October, 2164.
Windham's "perceptive introduction" did
not overcome Bone's disappointment in
the failure of the "fatuous" letters "to
provide insights into Williams' genius.
. . ."

E 102   Jack Sullivan, "Tennessee Williams'
Letters to Donald Windham, 1940-1965,
and Tanaquil," **Saturday Review** 5, 15
October, 35.
Sullivan said little about Windham's
editing of letters that had "an
extraordinary immediacy of emotion and
detail." **Tanaquil** was "an intentionally

low-keyed, almost muted novel, . . .
carefully and atmospherically developed"
around characters who "deserve a
livelier fate."

E 103   David Richards, "A Playwright's Early
Search for Art, Sex, Repose and Fame,"
Washington [D. C.] **Star**, 23 October.
This extended review of **Tennessee
Williams' Letters to Donald Windham,
1940-1965**, quoted verbatim passages from
an interview Richards conducted with
Windham, reflecting on both the friendship and the publication. The letters
themselves offered "a moving account of
an estrangement," according to the
reviewer. "As the years pass, you can
feel a bond slowly unraveling."

E 104   Frances Esmonde de Usabel, "Tanaquil,"
Library Journal 102, 15 November, 2371.
The "emotionally detached" narrative
about "two likeable people" was
"worthwhile but unexciting" to this
reviewer, who objected to Windham's
"consistent use of the past tense,"
whatever that meant.

E 105   Robert Brustein, "Tennessee Williams'
Letters to Donald Windham, 1940-1965,"
New York Times Book Review, 20 November,
9.
Expressing only grudging admiration for
Windham's editing, Brustein was ruthless
toward Williams: "The love that dared
not speak its name has now grown hoarse
from screaming it." He accused Windham
of "the shrill whistle of long-
suppressed rage," despite the "exculpa-
tory" and "sympathetic tone."

E 106   Pat Rosenberg, "Beautiful Illusions,
Lyric Parrot Soup," **Chicago Tribune**, 20
November.
"Old themes and cliches" in **Tanaquil**
seemed fresh to the reviewer. It was "a
novel of countless sophistications"
despite its having "over-romanticize[d]
youth, beauty, and a life in art."

E 107   Katha Pollit, "A Long Goodbye," **New York Times Book Review**, 27 November, 14.
Pollit disparaged the characterizations in **Tanquil** as "labels for narrative pawns" and dismissed the people as "bodiless."

E 108   Virgil Miller Newton, "Drama, Action Enliven Fall Books," **Tampa** [Florida] **Tribune**, 11 December.
Tanaquil, "an old-fashioned love story," had a "breathless intensity," and its hero, Frankie, was "a vague wonder."

E 109   Tim Dlugos, "Rough Trade, The Post Card as an Object of Art," **Christopher Street**, December, 53-54.
Dlugos briefly but favorably assessed Windham as a postcard collagist.

1978

E 110   Tennessee Williams, "Letter to the Editor," **New York Times Book Review**, 15 January, 14+18.
Pleading that he had worn the wrong glasses and been served "beef tongue and spinach, neither of which is at all palatable" to him, Williams attempted to deny he had given his permission to Campbell and Windham to publish his letters. He disparaged Windham's editing and "pitiably paranoic or savagely brutal" footnotes; he dropped names of other writers who were "brilliant" or "great"; he denied having had time to read the letters thoroughly in advance; he claimed coercion, even though the fact of dates undermined his efforts.

E 111   W. A. H. Kinnucan, "Tennessee Williams' Letters to Donald Windham 1940-1965, **New Republic** 178, 4 February, 38.
The reviewer accused Windham of "petulance," "repeated and judgmental references," and "self-congratulatory motives." He accused Williams of "unreliability."

E 112   Robert Brustein, "Letter to the Editor,"
         New York Times Book Review, 4 February,
         44-45.
         Brustein's response to Williams's letter
         [E110] and Windham's rejoinder to
         Brustein's review [C50] clarified his
         unsympathetic response to Windham and
         particularly to Williams.

E 113   David J. Leigh, "Tennessee Williams'
         Letters to Donald Windham, 1940-1965,"
         Best Sellers 37, March, 394-95.
         A "rambling and often boring account of
         25 years of 'striking poses on paper,'"
         the letters were in the main "trivial"
         or "sentimental," and valuable only as
         "resource material for a future psycho-
         history of Williams. Leigh found it "an
         unnecessary book" except for a few
         observations about literature and for
         Windham's introductions.

E 114   Tennessee Williams' Letters to Donald
         Windham, 1940-1965," **Choice** 15, March,
         75.
         Windham's editing, judged here as "self-
         pitying prefaces, footnotes, and asides,
         were simply disfiguring, and his inter-
         pretation of the finer points of these
         letters to the disadvantage of their
         author, some 30 years after their mail-
         ing, seems a little unsportsmanlike.
         Windham seems to have misapprehended the
         seriousness with which Williams regarded
         his craft."

E 115   Michelle Green, "His 'perfect friend'
         accused the author of planned intrigue
         and exploitation," **Atlanta Journal and
         Constitution Magazine**, 21 May, 10-11.
         This interview with Windham rehashed the
         review and exchange of letters in the
         New York Times Book Review summarized
         above [E 105, 110, 112].

E 116   Dotson Rader, "The Private Letters of
         Tennessee Williams," **London Magazine** 18,
         July, 18-28.

Ostensibly a review of **Tennessee Williams' Letters to Donald Windham, 1940-1965,** Rader's essay was instead an attack on Windham's integrity. Calling him "a scavenger of literary history, a peddler of privileged material," Rader then attempted to destroy his person and impugn his reputation by misusing passages from Williams's letters to support a number of defenseless accusations. He implied that the letters had been published without Williams's permission, and he assessed Windham's editing of the letters as "dishonest" and his commentary as "self-serving" and "arrogant." Rader seems not to have read either the letters or Windham's editorial apparatus carefully. He attacked Robert Brustein as well, for his review of the book [E105].

E 117   Selden Rodman, "Three Neurotics," **National Review** 30, 1 September, 1094. Allen Ginsberg and Dylan Thomas joined Williams in this review of private papers. Williams's letters, although "morally bankrupted," were "not devoid of gaiety and wit," and Windham had traced Williams's "fall from grace . . . with compassion."

1979

E 118   Phil Sanderlin, "Donald Windham Comes Home Again, Georgia Novelist's Collection Donated to University of Georgia Library," [University of Georgia] **Observer Exchange,** 6 December, 1-3B.
Incorporating passages from Robert Willingham Jr.'s biographical essay [E119], Sanderlin assessed Windham's gift of many of his books as manuscripts, as well as a substantial and impressive selection of inscribed or autographed books by other writers from both him and from Sandy Campbell: "a fine nucleus," as Willingham called it for the collection of contemporary

authors that the library was trying to build.

1980

E 119   Robert M. Willingham, Jr., "Donald Windham," **Dictionary of Literary Biography 6, American Novelists Since World War II**, Second Series, James E. Kibler, Jr., Editor. Detroit: Gale Research, Bruccoli Clark, 380-86.
This biographical essay, with illustrations, included some factual errors but offered a fair assessment of Windham's work.

1981

E 120   "Statement in Open Court," **London Magazine** 20, February-March. 80-81. Counsel to the editor of **London Magazine**, Alan Ross, and to the magazine as plaintiffs, acknowledged and apologized in summary for the lies and misleading quotations in Dotson Rader's review of **Tennessee Williams' Letters to Donald Windham 1940-1965** [E116].

E 121   Roy Fuller, et al, "London Magazine," [London] **Times Literary Supplement**, 13 February.
Fuller and eight other writers appealed to readers for funds to assist **London Magazine** in paying "a substantial bill for legal costs in a settled defamation action not of its seeking." Windham was not mentioned in the letter, although the defamation action over Dotson Rader's review of **Tennessee Williams' Letters to Donald Windham 1940-1965** was by inference the cause of the bill.

E 122   Alan Ross, "The 'London Magazine'," [London] **Times Literary Supplement**, 19 June.
Ross attacked Windham's letter [C54 in response to E121] as "a gratituous homily," and placing blame on contradictions in dates and claiming puzzlement that Windham, "ultimately so

disinterested in damages, should have
taken legal action in the first place."

E 123   Tim Dlugos, "His Dailiness: The Works of
Donald Windham," **Little Caesar 12:
Overlooked and Underrated.** Los Angeles:
Little Caesar Press, 63-67.
Calling on a line from Alice Notley's
poem, "His Dailiness" -- "not to be
anonymous, to love what's at hand" --
Dlugos's gracefully written, carefully
reasoned endorsement of Windham's work
offered an excellent defense of "as
 consistently fine a writer as any of his
generation." Concentrating, though not
exclusively, on **Two People**, Dlugos
called attention to Windham's unassum-
ing yet steady gaze" and his disincli-
nation to take the easy or the glib way
out. . . ."

1983

E 124   Robert Ferro, "Between the Covers," **Gay
News**, 4-10 February, 13.
After summarizing the complicated plot
of **Stone in the Hourglass** and its "world
of bad luck and random evil," Ferro
offered a wise assessment of one of the
"most intelligent, sensitive and, shame-
fully for us, unappreciated voices.
Fame-deserved has eluded him for 40
years, through which, nevertheless, he
has produced consistently rich and honest work. He has always lived in the
shadow of his better-known friends,
Tennessee and Truman, whose last names,
through fame, one needn't list. But
through the exigencies of drugs, liquor
and celebrity, it seems the time for
their contributions is over, while Mr.
Windham, who perhaps came in with a
marble or two less, still has all of
his, and happily many years more to
display his prodigious gifts."

E 125   Liz Smith, "Streisand is losing control
-- of 'Yentl'," **New York Daily News**, 16
June.

More a gossip's mongering than a
reviewer's assessment, Smith's commentary on **Footnote to a Friendship**
claimed that the book's "vitriol alone
might nudge it into a paperback
reprint." As "an almost unprecedented
paying off of old scores," the book was
"chock full of gossip and accusations,"
a "violent attack" on Capote's
"integrity, veracity and his work," and
"enough to turn even the most tolerant
person homophobic." Smith's assessment
indicates that she may have stared
harder at the photographs than at the
text.

E 126   Robert Ferro, "A Survivor's Look at the
        Damned," **Gay News Review of Books,** 27
        October, 1.
        Ferro perceived "something hangdog and
        neglected, sad and bewildered" in
        Footnote to a Friendship. It reflected
        "a writer's nightmare: hard work, no
        feedback or return, the delay of fame
        and approval -- all in the reflected
        glow cast by the enormous success of
        friends," although Windham did not
        "blame his obscurity on them or begrudge
        them their success."

1986

E 127   "Lost Friendships," **Kirkus** 54, 15
        December, 1854.
        "Love and honesty rule these twin por-
        traits of Capote and Williams, whose
        grotesque sea changes from hale com-
        panions to fearful gargoyles may never
        be so richly observed again." Windham
        was "always modest," and his "restraint"
        served him well, according to the
        reviewer, although the Williams section
        seemed more satisfying and therefore
        more conclusive. The whole book was
        nonetheless "vivid and heartfelt."

1987

E 128   "Lost Friendships," **Publisher's Weekly,**

16 January 65.
Following a brief summary of Windham's
memoir, the reviewer termed it "a
depressing account of wasted lives and
talents."

E 129   Michael Esposito, "Lost Friendships,"
Library Journal 112, 1 March, 78.
Windham's memoir was a "compelling
portrait," recommended for "collections
specializing in modern literature."

E 130   Dennis Drabelle, "Friends of Truman and
Tennessee," **USA Today**, 7 March, 4D.
In a joint review of **Truman Capote: Dear
Heart, Old Buddy** by John Malcolm Brin-
nin, and **Lost Friendships: A Memoir of
Truman Capote, Tennessee Williams, and
Others,** the reviewer notes (with misleading generalizations) that Windham's
friendships with the two subjects
"lasted through the '70s only to crumble
at the decade's end, when he became
embroiled in a lawsuit with Williams and
Capote took the latter's side." The
notice, however, was as much as about
Gore Vidal as it was about Windham's
book.

E 131   Andrew Holleran, "That Generation,"
Christopher Street 118, December, 3-7.
This lengthy, appreciative essay-review
of **Lost Friendships: A Memoir of Truman
Capote, Tennessee Williams, and Others**
constitutes the only serious attention
the book seems to have received.
Acknowledging the difficulties Windham
had to have encountered in maintaining
his objectivity, Holleran went on the
praise the tact in the writing as well
as its compassion.

E 132   **Letters of Carl Van Vechten**, Bruce
Kellner, Editor. New Haven: Yale
University Press.
This selection contains three letters to
Windham and four to Sandy Campbell with
references to Windham's writings.

Index

Books and publications appear in boldface.

About the Author

BRUCE KELLNER is Professor of English at Millersville University in Pennsylvania, where he teaches Shakespeare and Afro-American literature. He has published eight books, including *Carl Van Vechten and the Irreverent Decades* (1968), *The Harlem Renaissance: A Historical Dictionary for the Era* (Greenwood Press, 1984), *A Gertrude Stein Companion: Content With The Example* (Greenwood Press, 1988), and *The Last Dandy, Ralph Barton: American Artist, 1891-1931* (1991).